BELMONT UNIVERSITY LIBRARY
BELMONT UNIVERSITY
1900 BELMONT BLVD.
NASHVILLE, TN 37212

An Introduction to Christianity for a New Millennium

An Introduction to Christianity for a New Millennium

Scott Gambrill Sinclair

LEXINGTON BOOKS

A division of
ROWMAN & LITTLEFIELD PUBLISHERS, INC.
Lanham • Boulder • New York • Toronto • Plymouth, UK

LEXINGTON BOOKS

A division of Rowman & Littlefield Publishers, Inc.
A wholly owned subsidiary of The Rowman & Littlefield Publishing Group, Inc.
4501 Forbes Boulevard, Suite 200
Lanham, MD 20706

Estover Road
Plymouth PL6 7PY
United Kingdom

Copyright © 2008 by Lexington Books

All rights reserved. No part of this publication may be reproduced, stored in a retrieval system, or transmitted in any form or by any means, electronic, mechanical, photocopying, recording, or otherwise, without the prior permission of the publisher.

British Library Cataloguing in Publication Information Available

Library of Congress Cataloging-in-Publication Data

Sinclair, Scott Gambrill.
  An introduction to Christianity for a new millennium / Scott Gambrill Sinclair.
      p. cm.
  ISBN-13: 978-0-7391-2466-6 (cloth : alk. paper)
  ISBN-10: 0-7391-2466-8 (cloth : alk. paper)
  ISBN-13: 978-0-7391-2467-3 (pbk. : alk. paper)
  ISBN-10: 0-7391-2467-6 (pbk. : alk. paper)
  1. Christianity—21st century. I. Title. BR121.3.S56 2008
  230—dc22
                                                                          2007045420

Printed in the United States of America

∞™ The paper used in this publication meets the minimum requirements of American National Standard for Information Sciences—Permanence of Paper for Printed Library Materials, ANSI/NISO Z39.48-1992.

Dedicated to

Donald Gelpi, S.J.,

the greatest theologian of our time.

Contents

Acknowledgments	ix
Preface	xi

1. Creation in Genesis 1–2 and Subsequent Christian Thought — 1
2. The Fall, Noah, and the Understanding of "Sin" in Christian Tradition — 7
3. The Patriarchs and the Nature of Faith in Christian Tradition — 11
4. The Exodus and the Understanding of God in Christian Tradition — 15
5. Israel under the Judges and Kings; God as Visible in History — 21
6. Biblical Prophecy — 27
7. Biblical Wisdom, especially Job; Is God Just? — 33
8. Israel from the Exile until Jesus; Life after Death in Christian Tradition — 37
9. A Sketch of Jesus' Life and Personality — 43

10	The Birth of Jesus and the Doctrine of the Incarnation	49
11	The Baptism of Jesus and Baptism in Church History	53
12	The Teaching of Jesus	59
13	The Miracles of Jesus and Their Significance	65
14	The Eucharist in the Life of Jesus and Subsequently	73
15	The Death of Jesus and the Doctrine of the Atonement	81
16	The Historical Problem of Whether Jesus Rose from the Dead	91
17	The Significance of the Resurrection for the Early Church	97
18	The Taking of the Gospel to the Gentiles; Paul	103
19	Who Was Jesus and How Can We Know? John's Gospel	111
20	The Patristic Era	117
21	Monasticism	125
22	Three Major Types of Christianity	129
23	The Challenge of Modernity	141
24	The Feminine in Christian Tradition	147
25	Post-European Christianity	155
Index		159

Acknowledgments

I am profoundly indebted to friends who helped me. Here I can only mention a few of them by name. Donald Gelpi, S.J., read the entire first draft and made many corrections and suggestions. Prof. Harlan Stelmach read much of the book and made perceptive comments. Ms. Helen Knapp then found typographical errors and encouraged me. Dr. Roderick Dugliss and Dr. James Peters read a revised draft and suggested additional improvements. Since I did not always follow the advice of these wise and discerning friends, I bear sole responsibility for the defects that remain.

Preface

This book is intended to give a basic introduction to Christianity and is especially for people who have little knowledge of the topic. The book began as lecture notes for a survey course on Christianity, which I teach at Dominican University of California. I developed the course for students who came from non-Christian backgrounds. Later a friend urged me to turn the lectures into a short monograph. It is my hope that this book will serve as a suitable text for an introductory course in a college or seminary. The book could also be used for adult education in a church.

Christianity is vast and complex. It began with a series of historical experiences—especially the history of ancient Israel and the life of Jesus. These in turn generated a set of foundational documents—the Bible. Christians call the first major section of the Bible the "Old Testament." It is a collection of books in the Hebrew language and records the history and thought of the ancient Israelites—the people from whom Jesus came. The second section is the "New Testament" and is a collection of documents in Greek. These record the life and teaching of Jesus and the history and thought of the early church. From these experiences, especially as recorded in the Bible, a continuing culture emerged. That culture produced a theology, i.e., a set of beliefs about God and the meaning of human life. It also produced devotional practices and Christian institutions, such as the Papacy. Of course, there were art, music, and a long and complex history.

In this book we will survey important parts of this enormous heritage. We will especially go through major sections of the Christian Bible and review their basic contents and comment on the historical events that the Bible describes. We will look at the classical doctrines and most important rituals that emerged as Christians wrestled with the biblical material. We will briefly describe the major types of Christianity and the history that helped produce them.

In presenting the history of Christianity, I will emphasize the positive but will also note the negative. In my opinion, it is always best to emphasize achievements. Nevertheless, failures must be faced.

Throughout the book we will deal with the question of how to appropriate the Christian heritage today. I will share how I interpret the formative events and classical doctrines of the church and apply them to contemporary life. This interpretation and application will attempt to do justice both to the discoveries of modern science and scientific history and to the present social situation in the global village. My positions also arise out of my prayer life and personal relationship with God and experience as a priest in the Episcopal Church. It is my hope that an honest presentation of my views will help readers form their own independent understanding of what Christianity essentially is and how to respond to its claims today.

If there is an overall theme to this diverse book, it is that the center of Christianity is the death and resurrection of Jesus. Thus, in my opinion, Christianity is not primarily about the teaching of Jesus, as many Christian liberals assume, nor primarily about the Bible, as many Christian conservatives assume, nor primarily about the traditions of the church, as many devout Christians implicitly assume, nor primarily about the culture of a great religion, as non-Christians often assume—though, of course, all of these are important. Instead, the center of Christianity is the extraordinary claim that the man Jesus of Nazareth was executed and then raised from the dead by God, who through this act revealed that Jesus was divine. The Old Testament and the teaching of Jesus look forward to these astonishing events; the New Testament looks back on them; the traditions of the church begin with them and depend on them; the culture of Christianity in all its richness everywhere presupposes them and celebrates them. And, in my opinion, the truth of Christianity primarily depends on them and not on such things as the originality of Jesus' teaching or the overall accuracy of the Bible or the soundness of church dogmas. I will argue that we have access to the crucifixion and resurrection of Jesus through historical investigation and through personal spiritual experience and through the consequences of these events for understanding the meaning of human existence.

1

Creation in Genesis 1–2 and Subsequent Christian Thought

Lewis Carroll once made the charming observation that writers should begin at the beginning and when they get to the end should stop. The Bible follows this advice. It opens with the creation of the universe; and it concludes with the destruction of the present world and the appearance of a new and more blessed realm that will last forever.

Careful analysis shows that the Bible begins not with one account of creation but with two. The opening account describes the creation of the world in six days. In this story the universe begins as a dark, watery chaos, and God first creates light and divides the waters, producing the heaven and the earth and then the sea and the land. Subsequently God makes the plants and animals and finally human beings. On the seventh day God rests, and this rest becomes the basis for humanity observing a solemn weekly day of rest. The second story tells us of the creation of the first human beings, Adam and Eve, and the garden of Eden where they initially lived. In this story the earth seemingly begins as a barren plain, and God first creates a human being, Adam. Then God makes a wonderful garden, and in the process creates plants and animals. Finally, God creates a woman, Eve, out of Adam's rib. The garden is the source for the major rivers of the world.

These stories apparently once existed independently. It seems likely that the first creation story came out of an environment in which water was plentiful. It took an act of God to keep the water from overwhelming the land. God created the heavens and the earth and the dry land by *dividing* the waters. Perhaps a Jewish priest wrote this story in Babylon, which was on a river subject to severe flooding. As we will see, the Jewish priests who contributed to the Bible spent years in exile in Babylon. The priests were also anxious for people to keep the weekly Sabbath holiday, which the story justifies. By contrast, it seems likely that the second creation story came out of an environment in which water was scarce, since the story emphasizes that the garden paradise that God created was the source of the life-giving rivers that sustain the earth. Perhaps a lay person wrote this story in Jerusalem, the capital of the land in which the people of the Bible lived. Jerusalem and its surrounding lands are subject to drought.

An editor combined these differing stories to form the opening two chapters of what became the first book of the Bible, Genesis. I suspect that the editor took an older traditional story from Jerusalem and combined it with a more recent story from Babylon.

Because these stories are factually inconsistent, we must assume that at least the editor was not primarily concerned with factual consistency and did not believe that the details of the stories were literally true. It may be that the people who told the stories before the editor combined them thought that at least one account was factually accurate. Clearly, however, the editor who wrote down the narratives and placed them side by side must have noticed the inconsistencies. Apparently he was not concerned about them. He was not trying to give a "scientific" account of how the world began.

Nevertheless, these two stories are theologically consistent. In both stories there is only one God, and he is good. This God alone creates the world, and the world that he makes is good. The first story climaxes with the statement that God saw all that he had made and that it was very good. In the second story God begins by making a perfect garden full of fruit trees and abundant water. Both stories insist that human beings have a special relationship to God that the rest of the creation lacks. Part of this similarity involves lordship over creation. In the first account, God makes human beings in his own image and gives them dominion over the world. In the second account, God breathes his own breath into Adam, and Adam gives names to the animals. God then creates Eve, because the animals are not a suitable partner for the man.

God makes Eve out of Adam's side. Since she is Adam's flesh and bone, she shares in his dignity as a being who contains the very breath of God.

What is true of these opening stories is true of the Bible in general. The Bible is a mosaic of documents from different times and places and is often factually inconsistent. Nevertheless, the Bible tends to be theologically consistent, especially in maintaining such basic perspectives as ethical monotheism, the view that there is only one God, and he (the Bible usually pictures God in male imagery) is good.

Subsequent Christian thought built on the foundation of Genesis 1–2 to claim that God created the universe out of nothing. Genesis 1 opens with the words, "In the beginning God created the heavens and the earth." Genesis does not specify whether anything existed prior. Perhaps the author assumed that some amorphous stuff existed before the creation of the universe, much as modern astronomers hold that some unimaginable blob existed prior to the "Big Bang" that gave birth to the universe that we know. Genesis focuses on God "creating" the universe by bringing order out of primordial chaos. Nevertheless, Christians subsequently experienced that God was eternal and all other things were not. Consequently, they concluded that God must have created all things out of what had not previously existed. Here "all things" even include time and space, since these too are part of the universe.

Within Christian history the church's doctrine of creation has faced various competing theories. In biblical times the cultures surrounding the Jewish people were polytheistic and tended to portray the gods creating the world in a more grossly physical manner. A story from Mesopotamia tells us of a god making the universe out of the carcass of a primordial monster. A story from Egypt tells us of a god creating through masturbation, spitting, and weeping.

In the second and third centuries of the common era, the Gnostics claimed that some inferior spiritual being made the physical world by mistake and that the physical world is evil. Gnostics believed that the eternal Spiritual Principle was wholly immaterial and utterly "pure." This principle somehow produced other spiritual beings. One of the lowest was the Demiurge whose name literally means the "Craftsman." The Demiurge was ignorant and, as a result, produced the physical universe. Consequently, the material world is not the good creation of a wise and loving god. It is the mess produced by an incompetent. Enlightened people regard it with contempt and look forward to escaping from it at death.

In modern times, science has claimed that the universe, life, and human beings arose as a result of a huge series of cosmic coincidences. The present universe began with the enormous explosion of some primordial stuff. After the explosion, hydrogen atoms formed and coalesced into stars. Through thermonuclear reactions the stars produced heavier elements. From the resulting cosmic dust, the earth condensed. By accident organic molecules arose, and at least one of these came to life and was able to reproduce itself. Then life evolved through the natural selection of random mutations. Occasionally, a life form did not reproduce itself exactly. Most of these mutations were dysfunctional, and the resulting organisms did not survive. A few mutations were advantageous and enabled the resulting organisms to do better in their environments. These organisms became dominant. Thus, over billions of years some life forms became increasingly sophisticated. In relatively recent geological times, human beings came into existence. Consequently, we are the end result of billions of years of naturally selected accidents.

Today it does not seem necessary for a Christian to respond in detail to the polytheistic myths of Mesopotamia, Egypt, and elsewhere. These stories are the products of pre-scientific world views. We now know that the universe certainly did not begin with the carcass of a primordial monster or a god masturbating, spitting, and weeping.

The primary problem with the Gnostic claim that an incompetent god made the universe is that it is psychologically destructive. Perhaps it is plausible that an incompetent deity made the universe. Certainly the world that we know is—and, apparently, has always been—full of defects. The difficulty with the Gnostic view is that it forces us to think of our environment and even of our own bodies as essentially broken. The historical consequences of this attitude have been disastrous. It was the Gnostics who first taught, for example, that sex is dirty. The results of that mistake haunt us still.

To the Gnostic claim that the material universe is essentially evil, the Christian would reply that the present universe can be redeemed. Of course, in condemning the world as evil, Gnosticism focuses too much on the negative. The present universe teems with wonderful things. Nevertheless, it is clear that the present universe contains wrenching problems, and some of these are due to matter. Earthquakes, for example, cause enormous suffering and result from physical laws. The issue between Gnostics and orthodox Christians is whether the universe can be redeemed. Gnostics insist that it cannot be and, therefore, we should concentrate only on "spiritual" matters. The more optimistic Christian assumption that the universe can be redeemed has, of course, produced much material progress. For example, in response to the threat of earthquakes, we have developed technology that limits their harm.

The debate continues over whether the biblical world view or the scientific one is correct or whether they can somehow be combined. Christian Fundamentalists still claim that the biblical view is literally true. Unfortunately, they do not admit the existence of the contradictions in the biblical account(s) that the editor of Genesis already must have perceived. Atheistic reductionists, by contrast, dismiss as antiquated and naïve the Christian claim that the world is the product of a good creator.

It seems to me that in trying to resolve the debate, we should begin by noting that science and Christianity have different presuppositions. Modern science restricts its investigations to natural causation. Hence, claiming that God did something will never be "scientific." Of course, we must, therefore, remind ourselves that something might be true without being "scientific." Christianity starts with the experience of God in Christian history and in our own individual lives, and these experiences in turn change how we perceive the universe. Christians see God in the "creation." Moreover, the primary goal of Christians' lives is to have a relationship with God, and it seems incredible that the ability to enter into a relationship with God could result merely from billions of years of accidents.

As a Christian, I believe that God governs the world through law and through miracle. The universe has perceivable regularities. Some of these are natural, and some are psychological and social. Gravity is a natural law. Masses attract one another. The destructiveness of hatred is a moral law. When someone hates another person, the results are psychological dysfunction in the person who is full of the hatred and social tension between the two parties. The physical sciences investigate the natural laws; the social sciences investigate laws involving human psyches and organizations. I believe that such laws ultimately depend on God and reflect his goodness and that in most instances God allows them to continue uninterrupted. Nevertheless, as a Christian, I also hold that sometimes God makes special interventions in the universe. These we call miracles. The resurrection of Jesus (to be discussed later) is a prime example. Since we do not know as much as God does, we often cannot perceive why God works miracles at some times and not others. Nevertheless, as the resurrection illustrates, God does occasionally intervene on particularly important occasions. These important occasions serve as special signs that there is a God and that we should seek and serve him at all times.

Because God governs the universe partly through law, a Christian need not question the basic claims of science concerning the origins of the universe. Certainly, natural laws have determined much of what has happened. The universe that we know apparently did begin with the "Big Bang." Life did evolve over billions of years, and part of that process did occur through natural selection of random mutations. Consequently, some of what happened was accidental. Nevertheless, the "law" of natural selection does guarantee that some life would become more advanced. From a Christian perspective, this positive "evolution" was part of God's intent. Of course, such "natural" processes are all that science can hope to investigate and understand.

Nevertheless, because God also governs the universe partly through miracle, I suspect that at least some of the crucial events in the origin and evolution of the universe were due to special interventions by God. Perhaps one of these divine interventions was the "creation" of the first DNA molecule. As far as we know, all life depends on the DNA molecule, and the DNA molecule is fabulously intricate. There is no convincing "scientific" explanation of how the first DNA molecule could have arisen by accident. Perhaps one day there will be, but the claim that there must be a natural explanation is a gratuitous assumption. Of course, science will never be able to prove that God produced the first DNA molecule. At most, the lack of a scientific explanation will be a sign that God might have done so. The belief that God created the universe remains "faith." Faith depends on a personal relationship with God, which in turn is a response to the things that God has done in our individual lives and, especially, as we shall see, in Christian history.

2

The Fall, Noah, and the Understanding of "Sin" in Christian Tradition

After the two creation stories in Genesis 1–2, we have the story of the "fall" in Genesis 3. According to the story, God commands Adam and Eve not to eat fruit from the tree of the knowledge of good and evil and warns that the consequence will be death. The snake counters that the fruit will make them become like God himself. Adam and Eve eat of the fruit. They realize that they are naked and try to hide from God. God confronts them and demands to know if they have eaten from the forbidden fruit. Adam blames Eve, and Eve blames the snake. God punishes the snake by making it crawl on its belly and punishes Eve by making her subordinate to Adam and punishes Adam by making work drudgery. God also decrees that the couple and their descendants will be subject to death, and he drives Adam and Eve out of the garden of Eden. But before driving them out, God gives them clothes of skin to wear.

It would appear that the ancient author of this story did not intend to give a literal description of how sin, suffering, and death came into the world but a theological explanation for why these tragedies exist. Snakes do not talk, and the author apparently did not think that they once did. The story tells us that God punished the snake by making it slither, not by taking away its power of speech.

Theologically, the story insists that suffering results from the sin of human beings and other created things (e.g., snakes), not from the malicious will of an arbitrary God. Sin sometimes originates from our free choice to disobey God. Adam and Eve decided to disregard God's command. Nevertheless, sin is also a superhuman power at loose in history. Only the first human beings started with a clean slate. The rest of us inherit the consequences of the sin committed even before we were born. We die, because Adam sinned.

According to the story, the basic sin is the desire to escape the limitations of human existence by distrusting God and trying to become God ourselves. Before they disobeyed God, Adam and Eve had every blessing. They lived in a fabulous garden. Men and women were equal and trusted one another and work was not drudgery. Nevertheless, the serpent suggested that they lacked something and that if they only disobeyed God they could have it. What they lacked was the unlimited knowledge and power of God himself. The knowledge of "good and evil" that the snake promised was in all probability knowledge of everything, and knowledge bestows power. Adam and Eve defied God by trying to become God.

When we try to escape the limits of human existence, we realize our physical vulnerability and moral accountability, and we try to escape these by oppressing others. As long as we trust God, we are not overly anxious either about our physical safety or moral standing. We believe that God will somehow protect us, and we believe that God loves and forgives us. When we distrust God, we become anxious, and to alleviate our fear, we try to gain power over others so that they cannot threaten us. We also blame others for our own moral mistakes. The end result is that we end up being alienated from God, other people, and even our own selves. Despite our attempts to become secure, we are never fully secure, and in our efforts to gain power over others we make them insecure and hostile to us. Similarly, despite our attempts to blame others, we still know that often we are at fault.

From the story of the fall of Adam and Eve, Christian theology developed the doctrine of original sin. There are many variations on this doctrine, but basically it teaches that because of the fall, we are all subject to a spiritual disability. We are born into a sinful world, and from the very beginning of our lives this world distorts our values and molds our actions. Already as children, we imitate the ideals and behaviors of our sinful family, friends, and societies. These pre-existing misguided ideals and behaviors stem from even earlier history, ultimately going back to the first humans. Our wish to escape the limitations of being human especially distorts our desires. Instead of accepting the peace and joy that come from being centered to God, we are centered in ourselves and live for popularity or money or sex or alcohol and drugs. But since these things cannot be an adequate replacement for God's love, we feel that we never have enough of them, and we become obsessed with gaining more. Consequently, sin is a power beyond us that we cannot fully resist on our own. According to Christian teaching, we escape the otherwise irresistible pull of sin by submitting to baptism (a ceremony we will discuss later) and entering the church. There the supreme moral example of Jesus (see later discussion) and the power of God's Spirit are especially present.

There has been a major debate within Christian history over how seriously original sin undermines human freedom, especially in those outside of the church. More optimistic theologians have insisted that the effect of original sin is only moderate, and people can chose to lead virtuous lives totally apart from becoming baptized Christians. More pessimistic theologians have held that, apart from the grace which comes from baptism and inclusion in the church, human beings can only sin. Some extremely pessimistic theologians have claimed that even Christians cannot overcome the pull of original sin but simply must rely completely on the undeserved mercy of God.

In my opinion, all these theories are basically correct but apply in different situations. Probably the majority of people in most circumstances can choose to do what is right without being Christian or even having any religious orientation. The world is full of ethical people who are not religious. Sometimes, however, people need faith in God and the spiritual support of the church or some similar organization, such as Alcoholics Anonymous (AA), to break patterns of destructive behavior. Without believing in a higher power and attending AA meetings, many alcoholics cannot stop drinking. And probably most people have at least a few destructive "compulsions" that they cannot overcome under any circumstances. In the face of such irresistible "bad habits," we must rely on the assurance that God loves and forgives us despite our inability to improve.

After the story of the fall of Adam and Eve, the Bible has a series of stories about how evil multiplied, and the most famous of these is Noah and the Ark in Genesis 6–9. According to the biblical account, human beings had illicit sex with angels and committed other atrocious acts. God resolved to destroy humanity. Nevertheless, he had mercy on a righteous man named Noah. God told him to build a great ship and to put his family and breeding pairs of every type of animal on it. Then God sent a great flood that destroyed all other sentient beings. When the flood abated, God promised never again to destroy the earth and gave the rainbow as a sign of his pledge. He also allowed human beings the right to eat meat and restrained unlimited violence by instituting the law of (limited) vengeance: Whoever kills a human being will be killed.

These later biblical narratives follow a pattern. Human beings sin by trying to usurp the rights that belong to God alone. For example, in the Noah story when human beings have sex with angels, the distinction between the human and the divine realm is broken. God then punishes human beings. In the Noah story, God decides to destroy the world with a flood. Nevertheless, God moderates the punishment. For example, he chooses Noah, has him put samples of all animals on a ship, and they survive.

Of course, this pattern already appears in the story of the fall. Adam and Eve ate the fruit in the hope of becoming like God. God punished them but also mercifully gave them clothes of skin.

Underlying this pattern is an understanding of how God deals with sin. God punishes sin because he is just. Nevertheless, God punishes our sins less than they deserve, because he is merciful. God takes the initiative in trying to restore his relationship to human beings who have disobeyed him.

The doctrine that God is both just and merciful and takes the initiative in trying to restore his relationship to errant human beings is central to the whole Bible and subsequent Christian thought.

Today the story of Noah has taken on a new meaning in the context of the ecological crisis. The ecological crisis has recently become much more severe due to such things as global warming and the massive destruction of natural habitats. One especially troubling dimension of the crisis is the expanding number of extinctions. The Noah story powerfully claims that God, who created all species, continues to care about their preservation. He calls us to take action in his behalf to save them from the consequences of human wrongdoing.

3

The Patriarchs and the Nature of Faith in Christian Tradition

After the stories of the spread of sin in Genesis 1–11, the Bible begins a history of a single people—the Israelites. At the start of this history, we have a saga of the family from which the Bible records that the Israelites descended. Specifically, we trace the family through four generations of leaders (often called "Patriarchs"): Abraham, Isaac, Jacob—who is given the name "Israel"—and Jacob's twelve sons, who become the founders of the subsequent twelve tribes of Israel. In the stories, Abraham, Isaac, Jacob, and his sons are shepherds who wander from place to place, especially in what we now call Israel or Palestine. God repeatedly appears to the patriarchs and promises to give them this land and to make their descendants a great nation. God also commands them to do various things. Of course, the shepherds have to believe the promises and obey the commands for the promises to take effect.

It is difficult to determine how much of these stories actually happened. On the one hand, the stories are not for the most part fantastic, and we would not expect that contemporary historical records would normally mention "family" events. On the other hand, the biblical accounts were written down centuries later and reflect subsequent theological and historical developments. Thus, the claim that the twelve tribes of ancient Israel descended from a single individual seems to be a poetic way of explaining ethnic relationships to a subsequent time. The claim teaches that these tribes somehow share a common historical origin, and this shared past should facilitate their cooperation in the present.

The stories of the Patriarchs have a theology of election and faith. God chooses certain persons to have a special role in larger history. He somehow reveals himself to them and commands them to break with their past and do something new. The recipient of the revelation must trust God and obey. The commands that God gives sometimes seem impossible or irrational. Nevertheless, God guides history and things work out.

Perhaps the most irrational story about the Patriarchs is the sacrifice of Isaac in Genesis 22. Despite the fact that Abraham and his wife Sarah are too old to have children and Sarah is sterile, God promises that Abraham will have a son. Abraham believes, and his son Isaac is born. Then, however, God tests Abraham by ordering him to offer Isaac as a human sacrifice. Abraham prepares to do so. God rescinds the order at the last possible moment, and since Abraham has passed the test, God renews the promise that Abraham will be the ancestor of a great nation.

In subsequent thought Abraham serves as a model for faith. Indeed, Abraham becomes the model for someone who abandoned false divinities and was faithful to the one true God, though the Bible does not explicitly say that Abraham was a monotheist. Partly because of this later tradition that he was a monotheist, Abraham became a hero that the three great Western monotheistic religions, Judaism, Christianity, and Islam, share. We are all "Abrahamic faiths." In the New Testament, Abraham is especially the model for someone who trusted God, even when it seemed irrational to do so. For example, Paul wrote to the Romans that "when it was hopeless, so he might have hope, he [Abraham] trusted that he would become the 'father of many nations'" (Romans 4:18).

As the story of Abraham illustrates, faith is necessary because our blindness can make God's call to us seem impossible. Because of the effects of original sin and our own freely chosen sin, we become captives of sin and cannot do the things that are required. God intervenes by appearing to us and giving us the promise of his undeserved love. With that promise he gives us an empowering command to do something new that will help our lives move forward and bring salvation to others. Because of our blindness due to sin, the promise and the command can seem irrational. Nevertheless, we must trust God and obey. If we do, things work out by divine providence, though normally not without suffering and struggle on our part.

An important issue is how we discern God's call in the midst of all our irrational impulses. We have many daydreams about ourselves accomplishing heroic things, and most of these fantasies are both ridiculous and egoistic. Because of all these daydreams, it is often psychologically difficult to discern when God is calling us to do something that also seems impossible.

Christianity would insist that there are principles that enable us to separate God's summons from our own foolish impulses. Specifically, God's call gives us peace and makes us more loving. It can be at least partially verified by other Christians who are spiritually sensitive and mature. We can also verify it in our own experience as we grow in our relationship with God and others.

An implication of the Christian doctrine of faith is that our essential identity is not who we happen to be presently but who we can become through responding to God's call. Who we happen to be at any moment is partly the result of accident—and of sin. Our essential identity is what God, who is responsible for our creation, intends for us to become.

We come to know this identity not primarily by looking at ourselves but by looking at the role models that God gives, especially Jesus. Looking at ourselves as we presently are can be misleading. It focuses our attention on many things that are accidental and unhelpful. Moreover, accurate self-knowledge is often depressing. An honest inventory of ourselves inevitably reveals much that is broken or even disgusting. To grow, we must instead focus on illustrations of who we will become if we surrender to God's empowering call. The supreme illustration is Jesus himself, who is simultaneously the definitive revelation of who God is and who a human being can become through God's grace. Of course, the saints down through the ages provide other illustrations of lives transformed by God's indwelling Spirit. Some of these saints are in our own communities and provide "role models" that we can actually meet.

A further implication of the Christian doctrine of faith is that our primary knowledge of God will come in the future. At present we know God only dimly, because our perception of God is clouded by our own ignorance and sin. Now we must follow God, trusting that our relationship with him will grow and our perception of him will deepen. This growing relationship will culminate in perfect knowledge when we enter into eternal life.

4
✛
The Exodus and the Understanding of God in Christian Tradition

After the stories of the Patriarchs, the book of Exodus tells us that the Israelites fall into slavery in Egypt. At the end of Genesis, Jacob and his sons with their families travel to Egypt to escape a famine. They come at the invitation of the Egyptian Pharaoh and at first fare well. Then, however, Exodus informs us that there is a change in regime. The new Pharaoh reduces the Israelites to slavery, and they must work making bricks.

God responds by sending a man named Moses to liberate them. Moses is born from Jewish parents and grows up in Egypt but then flees to a foreign country. There God appears to Moses and reveals that his divine name is "Yahweh," which the Bible relates to the verb to be ("haya"). God commands Moses to go down to Egypt and liberate the Israelites.

God sends an escalating series of calamities on the Egyptians that allow the Israelites to depart. To force the Egyptians to free his people, God strikes the Egyptians with such things as gnats, hail, and locusts. At first, Pharaoh remains obdurate. God sends a final plague that kills all the first-born children of Egypt. In connection with this plague, God commands the Israelites to celebrate an annual holiday, the Passover, to commemorate the fact that God "passed over" the Israelites and only slew the Egyptian first born. Pharaoh finally lets the Israelites depart. Then he changes his mind and leads his army in pursuit. God divides the "Reed Sea" so the

Israelites can flee through it. But when the Egyptians attempt to follow, God causes the water to return, and the Egyptians drown. The Israelites escape into the desert, where God miraculously provides food and water.

God then makes a covenant with the Israelites. The Israelites come to Mount Sinai. God majestically appears and through Moses, God and the Israelites make a solemn commitment to one another. They will be his chosen people and must keep his law, which he then reveals.

The special law that God gives the Israelites basically mandates four things. First, the Israelites must worship only Yahweh. The Israelites cannot worship other deities. The first and, apparently, most important commandment is that the Israelites can have no other God. Second, the Israelites must be just to one another and merciful to the poor and the vulnerable. God is concerned about the well-being of every Israelite. Of course, the marginal especially need protection, and God gives regulations to benefit them. Third, the Israelites will perform certain cultic practices. To perform these, the Israelites must construct the "tabernacle," a sacred tent, and the "ark," a box that contains sacred objects. The Bible describes the tabernacle and ark in detail and claims that in some sense they are God's dwelling place. Theologically, what is most important about them is that they are portable. God travels with his people. Finally, the Israelites will observe what we would call an ethnic lifestyle. They will eat only certain things, dress in a special way, keep certain holidays.

Within the Old Testament, the Exodus is the central event. The stories of the patriarchs look forward to it. For example, in Genesis 15:12–16 God reveals to Abraham that his descendants will serve as slaves in a foreign land but then God will liberate them. At the end of Genesis, the Israelites actually arrive in Egypt, and yet there is the prediction that one day God will bring them back to the land he promised to give them (e.g., Gen. 50:24). Subsequent biblical books look back on the Exodus. For example, the prophetic books constantly criticize the Israelites for not being faithful to the stipulations of the covenant that they made with God. Even more important, the biblical text locates the entire basis of Israelite religion and life in the events that make up the Exodus, since during it the Israelites receive both their law and worship. Moreover, it is in the

Exodus that we first encounter Israel as a people rather than an extended family.

In the Exodus narrative God reveals who he is. Genesis often presupposes what God is like, but in the text God never reveals his divine nature to the characters in the stories. By contrast in Exodus chapter 3 and chapter 6, God reveals his name, and in the Bible a name signifies someone's essence. Specifically, God is ethical and especially concerned about the oppressed. He is also transcendent and cannot be identified with a natural phenomenon (e.g., the sun), a place, or an image. According to the text, his name means that he simply "is," and God specifically forbids the Israelites from trying to represent him with a statue (an "idol"). Because he is transcendent, he must reveal himself in order for him to be known at all. Finally, God is jealous. He cannot tolerate his people worshiping other deities and demands that they place loyalty to him above all other concerns.

Even as the Exodus account emphasizes the greatness of God and the fact that he made a covenant with the Israelites, it also emphasizes the weakness and unreliability of the people he summons. They continually doubt him and turn away. In response to their desert hardships, the Israelites long to return to the security of slavery in Egypt. The Israelites also anger God by making a golden calf in an attempt to represent him, and Moses must destroy the idol.

While the difference between this religious system in Exodus and that of surrounding ancient cultures can be exaggerated, it is real. In the ancient world the gods do demand justice and have some concern for the poor. Even monotheism appears occasionally. Nevertheless, Exodus's extreme emphasis that one must not make an image of God and that God is especially concerned about the marginal seems unique. In addition, there do not appear to be any parallels to the Israelite claim that the relationship between a nation and its God began with a voluntary covenant.

The narrative of the Exodus appears to be a highly overstated retelling of a series of historical events. The narrative certainly exaggerates God's wonders (e.g., the plagues) to emphasize his greatness. Surviving Egyptian texts make no mention of the Exodus. Nevertheless, there is probably a historical core. It seems unlikely that the Israelites would have invented the embarrassing fact that they were descended from slaves. One of the pharaohs during the

Exodus period was probably Ramesses II (13th c. B.C.E.). He enslaved Semites and used them in huge building projects, including the construction of his capital Ramesses, which the Bible mentions explicitly (Exod. 1:11). A group of slaves apparently managed to escape into the desert, thanks to the "miracle" of the Reed Sea. Perhaps the miracle occurred when the wind drove back marshy water and then let it return (Exod. 14:21, 28). The Israelites were able to continue on foot, and the more heavily armored Egyptians could not pursue. In the desert the escapees adopted a new religion, which at least was the forerunner of later Israelite faith. Then they made their way into the hill country of Palestine. It is noteworthy that an inscription from Ramesses II's successor, Merneptah, records the defeat of "Israel" during a military campaign there. This is the first mention of Israel outside the biblical narrative and proves that some people by that name had already come into existence, perhaps recently.

Mosaic religion became the foundation for subsequent Judaism, which retained its major features. Judaism has ever after been centered in the study of the Mosaic Law. Even today conservative Jews debate how to spell out the requirements of the ancient regulations and apply them to modern life. The detailed application gives to Judaism much of its distinctive character, including its food, dress, and holidays. The law also gives to Judaism its special sense of the sacredness of everyday life, since all of life is an attempt to embody the revealed will of God.

In my opinion, the most profound of all the ideas in Exodus is the insistence that God has no limits but is personal. God simply "is" and has no boundaries. He is present in all times and places. Yet, he is loving, and part of this love is an intimate knowledge of who we are and a challenge to us to become better. In contrast to God, all other personal beings seem to have limits. For example, a human person is always in a particular place at a particular time. Aside from God, our experiences of things that are limitless are vague and impersonal. Often we have such experiences when we are somehow disoriented. When we enter into God's presence, perhaps through prayer and meditation, our sense of time and space tends to fall away. Nevertheless, we experience that the reality we encounter loves us deeply, knows us completely, and calls us to grow.

Because God is personal, the Bible insists that we have an obligation to love him. God cares about our attitudes toward him, and, consequently, it is not enough merely to act ethically toward other human beings. Instead, we must also honor and cherish God himself. Indeed, the biblical book of Deuteronomy emphasizes that we must love God with all our being (Deut. 6:5), and Jesus taught that this was the first and greatest commandment (Mark 12:29–30). Our acts of love toward other human beings are themselves an expression of our love for God. God cares about everyone whom he has created, and our love for God impels us to reach out to all.

Christianity made important alterations in Mosaic religion. While retaining monotheism, Christianity insists that the one God exists in three "persons," and one of these became a human being (the incarnation and the Trinity are discussed later). While retaining the "ethical" regulations in the Mosaic Law, Christianity dropped the ethnic ones. Christianity insists that we must treat others lovingly, but we do not need to keep a special diet or dress code. Christianity also claims that in Jesus God made a "new covenant" that supersedes the Mosaic one. This new covenant was not with an ethnic people but with the church, the community that accepts Jesus as the definitive revelation of God. Hence, for Christians the symbolic dwelling place of God is not the ark (or the temple in Jerusalem where it resided until the ark's destruction). Instead, God dwelt in the flesh of Jesus and now especially dwells in the church. Christian art mostly dropped the Jewish prohibition of making images of God. Eastern Christianity allows artists to paint God in the forms, such as a burning bush or an angel, that he took to reveal himself in some of the biblical stories. Western Christianity even allows images of God himself. A particularly famous example is the series of paintings by Michelangelo illustrating God creating the world and Adam and Eve.

Partly because of these changes, the church views Moses primarily as a forerunner of Jesus. We can see an illustration of this attitude in a New Testament story which is called the Transfiguration (Matt. 17:1–13, Mark 9:2–13, Luke 9:28–36). In this story Jesus takes his closest disciples to the top of a mountain. There his clothes become unearthly white, and Moses appears along with the great prophet Elijah. One of Jesus' disciples suggests making three shrines to honor these three luminaries. Then a voice from heaven insists that the disciples should listen to Jesus. The implication is obvious: As great as Moses was, we must concentrate on Jesus.

In contemporary Christianity, Moses and the Exodus especially function as reminders that we must work to liberate the oppressed. Christians are continually tempted to think that our religion is only about inner relationships to God or the performance of sacred rituals. The story of Moses contradicts this delusion. God is just, is especially concerned about the marginal, and summons us to set people free. Fortunately, many Christians down through the ages, such as the abolitionists in the nineteenth century United States or Archbishop Desmond Tutu in twentieth-century South Africa, have responded courageously to God's summons and helped produce just societies.

Nevertheless, Christians also must remember that Jesus gives us a wider vision of who the oppressed are. In Exodus the oppressed are primarily God's chosen people who are suffering unjustly. By contrast, in the New Testament, the oppressed include all people who are suffering, regardless of the reason. Jesus was primarily concerned about mercy, and he declared that he came to save sinners (Mark 2:17).

5

Israel under the Judges and Kings; God as Visible in History

Much of the Old Testament after the book of Exodus concerns the history of the Israelites (later called the Jews). Here we summarize the period from around 1200 B.C.E. until 586 B.C.E. and compare the biblical record with what a modern historian might conclude "actually" happened.

According to the Bible, after the Israelites disobey God, he punishes them by making them wander in the desert. When they escape from Egypt, God initially invites the Israelites to enter Palestine and conquer it. They cower because of the strong forces defending it. God decrees that, because of its lack of faith, that generation will not enter the promised land; only their descendants will. The Israelites subsequently spend forty years wandering about in the wilderness. God sustains them by miraculously providing food and water. At the end of this period Moses dies.

It is difficult for modern scholarship to evaluate all this, but it seems that the Bible gives an exaggerated account of what occurred. If hundreds of thousands of people wandered through the desert for decades, as the Bible claims, there would surely be archaeological remains. No such remains have been found. Probably only a small number of people traveled through the desert, and they were not there nearly as long as the Bible records. Nevertheless, it seems likely that at least a few people did actually journey from Egypt to Palestine. Not only does the Bible claim that there was such a group, but in addition, several of the major characters, beginning with Moses himself, have Egyptian names. Once again the Bible remembers a historical event but exaggerates it in order to express its larger theology that God is great and guides key events in history. It is also worth noting that many of the "miracles" that the Bible describes (e.g., obtaining water by striking a rock; Num. 20:9–11) appear to be heightened accounts of natural phenomena in the area that lies between Egypt and Palestine.

According to the Bible, the Israelites then invaded Canaan (modern Palestine) and conquered it, but the Bible gives conflicting accounts about the details. In the opening chapters of the book of Joshua, all the tribes of Israel working together under the leadership of Joshua quickly overwhelm the entire land. By contrast in the first chapter of the following book of Judges, the tribes conduct individual campaigns and often make only limited gains.

Modern archeology suggests that Israel arose when people migrated from the Canaanite cities into the hills of Palestine and came to a new ethnic identity. The physical remains indicate that around 1200 B.C.E. the Canaanite cities were in decline. Meanwhile, the number of villages in the hill country soared. In such things as pottery, architecture, and alphabet, these new settlements show a great continuity with the Canaanite cities, but on a lower economic level. Accordingly, it appears that in a period of urban decay, people left the lowlands and homesteaded in the hills. There, we must assume, they associated with old-timers and with small groups of foreign immigrants, including some recent escapees from Egypt. Out of this mix, a new national identity formed, which we call "Israel." Ultimately, this new "nation" came into conflict with the Canaanite cities from which most of the inhabitants had come.

The origins of Israel helped produce the theology that God is on the side of the oppressed. The immigrants from the Canaanite cities were presumably fleeing from poverty and probably also from an oppressive hierarchical society. In the hills they gained new independence. Then a group of former slaves arrived from Egypt. These preached that their God was stronger than the gods of Egypt and had defeated them in the miracle of the sea. This God was the patron not of the rich and the powerful, but of the marginal. He was concerned about the poor and the widow and the resident alien. The new immigrants from the cities undoubtedly found this theology congenial.

Nevertheless, the endurance of the idea that God is on the side of the oppressed resulted primarily from its ethical superiority and its consonance with continuing religious experience. As we shall see, Israel soon became a monarchy, and the rich and the powerful dominated much of subsequent Christian history. Not surprisingly, the church often became subservient and proclaimed that God supported the elite and that their very wealth and power were signs of his favor. Yet the conviction that God is primarily concerned about the marginal has continually revived. The reason for its survival is both ethical and experiential. Ethically, a loving God should be concerned about all his children, and especially concerned about those who are in greatest need. Experientially, the poor and those who have ministered to them have always felt God's compassion, and this compassion has in turn summoned them to struggle against oppressive systems. Of course, the biblical theology that God is the champion of the poor has greatly aided this struggle.

The fact that historically, Israel emerged mostly through peaceful immigration allows us to put some disturbing material in the book of Joshua into a more helpful perspective. The book of Joshua insists that God commanded the Israelites not only to conquer the people of Canaan (modern Palestine) but also to exterminate them lest the Israelites adopt their religious practices. Today any ethically sensitive person would reject a religion that holds that God would ever demand genocide. In fact, however, the book of Joshua itself does not advocate genocide. The book was written centuries after the rise of Israel and was opposing subsequent Israelite assimilation of native Canaanite religious practices, such as worshiping the goddess of sexual love. The book expressed its theology by insisting that it was Yahweh who had given the Israelites their land and had commanded them to exterminate debased religion there. We may regret that the author chose to illustrate his message in such a violent way. However, I personally would agree that various religious practices, including worshiping sex, are destructive and contrary to God's will.

According to the Bible, after becoming established in Canaan, the Israelites went through a series of historical cycles during the era of the "judges." The book that bears the name "Judges" presses the history into a pattern. The Israelites forsake God by worshiping other gods. God punishes them by allowing an enemy to oppress them. The Israelites plead for mercy. In response God raises up a hero (called a "judge") who rallies the Israelites and with God's help defeats the enemy.

Modern scholarship suggests that this historical portrait may well be basically accurate. To be sure, the stories were written down centuries afterward and impose an artificial theological unity on the material. Nevertheless, the overall impression that Judges gives fits what we know. During the early history of Israel, the nation was decentralized, consisting of independent tribes. In such a situation, temporary charismatic leadership would repeatedly have arisen to deal with military crises. Hence, Israel probably went through periods of oppression followed by the rise of a "judge" who, no doubt in the name of the national God, rallied the tribes and liberated people.

The Bible goes on to describe the long period of the monarchy. In the biblical record, the Israelites demand a king, and God agrees to provide one. The first king, Saul, sins and loses God's favor and dies in battle. God chooses a new king, David. The Bible spends much time describing David's life and dwells both on his military achievements and on his personal sins, including committing adultery with another man's wife and having the husband murdered. David's son Solomon succeeds him, and the Bible portrays him as supremely wealthy and wise. Nevertheless, Solomon accommodates the religious practices of his many foreign wives, and God punishes Israel by initiating revolts during Solomon's time and dividing the kingdom after his death. Shortly after Solomon's demise, the northern and larger part of the kingdom secedes and remains independent for two centuries. In 722 the Assyrian Empire conquers this Northern Kingdom, and it disappears from history. The Southern Kingdom ("Judah") survives until 586 when the Babylonian Empire destroys it and takes its leading citizens into exile.

In describing the long histories of the two kingdoms, the Bible claims that when their kings are loyal to God, the nations prosper, but when they abandon God, he punishes them. The Bible also insists that the eventual destruction of both kingdoms is divine retribution for their sins.

By contrast, modern scholarship suggests that the evolution of the monarchy primarily reflected international politics. The monarchy arose to coordinate military defense against the Philistines, who were more powerful than previous invaders. The success of

David and Solomon was primarily due to a power vacuum in the larger Middle East, and in any case, the Bible exaggerates their achievements. The primary cause of the ultimate destruction of the two kingdoms was the renewed power of the Assyrian Empire, which destroyed the Northern Kingdom and the later rise of the Babylonian Empire, which destroyed the southern one.

The Bible holds that we encounter God in the events of history. Of course, the Bible acknowledges that we also see the glory of God in nature and in our own hearts. Nevertheless, the Bible stresses that we especially see God at work in events, and the Bible itself is primarily a religious interpretation of more than a millennium of history.

Unfortunately, much of the Bible tends to impose a simplistic theological model on history. It is not the case that godly rulers always have military and economic success and ungodly ones always produce national catastrophe. Even a careful reading of the biblical material itself demonstrates that sometimes there is no correlation between national virtue and political well-being. Thus, for example, the Bible claims that it was the supreme wickedness of King Manasseh that made God decide to destroy the Judah (2 Kings 21:10–16) and that the subsequent righteousness of King Josiah made God postpone the destruction until after his death (2 Kings 22:14–20). Nevertheless, the Bible also records that Manasseh had the longest reign of any king of Judah and died in his bed, whereas Josiah was slain in battle!

As a Christian, I would agree that God does reveal himself through history (both of nations and individuals) but that often a great deal of perception is required to see him. Certainly a discerning look at human events does show that lies are exposed and the truth does come to light, that oppressive policies do produce resistance and righteous ones do foster peace, that institutions founded on spiritual values often endure. But, of course, there are exceptions, and in the short run it can seem that mere chance or even heinous evil triumph.

6

✣

Biblical Prophecy

A large portion of the Old Testament consists of "prophecy." Specifically, we have three long books, Isaiah, Jeremiah, and Ezekiel, that have traditionally been known as the "major prophets." We also have twelve shorter books that have traditionally been known as the "minor prophets." In addition, stories about what "prophets" did and said appear elsewhere in the Bible.

The biblical "prophet" looks into the heart of God and then reveals God's perspective to his people. The Bible sometimes pictures God consulting with his angelic advisers and the prophet listening in. Or by the power of God's Spirit the prophet shares in God's own anger or compassion. Then the prophet reveals to the Israelites God's judgment and in the name of God demands that people respond appropriately. For example, the prophet may proclaim that God is angry because the Israelites are worshiping other deities and are oppressing the poor. On behalf of God, the prophet demands that the people repent. Consequently, biblical prophecy is basically inspired preaching. The prophet discerns the "voice" of God and makes it heard.

When biblical prophecy tells us about the future, it does so by discerning what God will do in response to the current situation or to promote his larger plan of salvation. The biblical God insists that he will somehow punish the Israelites if they are wicked and will somehow reward them if they are righteous. In response to a specific situation that is unjust, the prophet predicts that God will send a drought or a plague or a foreign invasion. Or in response to Israel's faithfulness to God's commands, the prophet predicts that God will send the blessings of prosperity and victory. Yet, in the midst of God's response to present behavior, there is a continuing divine plan to bring salvation to his people and to the larger world. As a result, even when prophets pronounce disaster, they sometimes look forward to later blessings, especially to God dwelling definitively among his chosen people forever and through his people bringing lasting peace and justice to the world.

As the Israelites and then the early Christians experienced God in new ways, they perceived new dimensions in older biblical passages (not all of which had originally been predictions) and saw these passages as somehow announcing the events of a much later period. Christians especially have held that the Old Testament prophets foresaw the coming of Jesus, his death and resurrection, and the rise of the church.

Today we would doubt that the prophets foresaw these events in a simplistic way, but some of the concerns of the prophets do point forward to Jesus and the church. Like most human predictions, biblical prophecies tended to be concerned about the immediate future, not about what would happen centuries later. And like all human predictions, biblical prophecies did not always turn out to be fully accurate. Nevertheless, biblical prophecy was based on larger ethical principles and on a vision of a divine plan to save God's people and the rest of the world. Consequently, some of the predictions hinted at the spiritual breakthroughs of a later era. The prophets hoped for a new age in which God would dwell in the midst of his people and through them the world would come to know him. As a Christian, I would hold that this hope points forward to the coming of Jesus, his death and resurrection, and the rise of the church.

From what we have seen, it is clear that biblical prophecy must be distinguished both from fortune telling and forecasts. We may define fortune telling as predicting the future through the occult. The fortune teller has esoteric techniques (e.g., reading palms) that reveal what must take place. An implication is that the future is already arbitrarily fixed and there are special avenues through which we can discover what it must be. We may define forecasts as predicting the future by looking at tendencies visible now. For example, we look at present meteorological conditions and project how they will evolve. An implication is that the present situation already dictates what the future will be. In general the Bible forbids using the occult and does not hold that present tendencies allow us to know the future. Only God gives such knowledge.

To get a taste of biblical prophecy, we can consider two prophets in the eighth century B.C.E., Amos and Hosea. The prophet Amos proclaimed that God was angry over social injustice in the Northern Kingdom and was demanding repentance, and Amos accurately predicted the nation's destruction. Amos lived in a brief period of renewed Israelite power and prosperity before the invasions of Assyria in the middle of the century. Because of the favorable political and economic circumstances, the rich were enthusiastic about the worship of the national God. Unhappily, the rich also used their increased economic power to exploit the poor even more than previously. In response, Amos insisted that God was enraged over the unethical treatment of the poor and, as a result, found Israel's worship offensive. Instead of fancy liturgies, God demanded social justice for the needy. Amos also insisted that God would destroy the nation because of its sins. Nevertheless, the nation should repent so that God would be merciful to the survivors. Subsequently, Amos's predictions proved to be correct. Assyria did indeed conquer the Northern Kingdom and deport its people, and Northern Israel disappeared from history.

Hosea proclaimed that Israel's worship of other deities was making Yahweh jealous, and he would take action. Hosea prophesied a few years later than Amos, and the Assyrian invasions were already drastically weakening the Northern Kingdom. During this period most Israelites were combining the worship of Yahweh with that of Baal, the Canaanite god of thunder and fertility. Hosea portrayed God as feeling the way that a loving husband feels when his wife is committing adultery. Hosea insisted that God would punish Israel severely and yet longed to have her back and, hence, would ultimately restore her to favor. Of course, after Assyria destroyed the Northern Kingdom, the Southern Kingdom (Judah) did survive and continued to play a role in God's "plan" to save the Jewish people and the rest of the world.

We may note that today many Christians, including myself, remain enthusiastic about some of the basic ideas in Amos and Hosea. Certainly Amos' proclamation that God is outraged over the exploitation of the poor was not only true in his day but is always profoundly true. God feels the suffering of humanity and is dismayed at the sin that produces it. Hosea's proclamation that God loves us with the passion of a jealous husband rightly stresses that God loves us more deeply than any human being does and demands that we place loyalty to him before all other loyalties. Moreover, only our relationship with God can bring us eternal joy.

Perhaps the most famous story about the prophets is the small book of Jonah, which we can summarize briefly. God tells Jonah to go to the notorious Pagan city of Nineveh and proclaim its sins. Instead of doing so, Jonah sails away toward Tarshish (a city in Spain?). God responds by sending a violent storm that threatens to destroy the ship. The Pagan sailors pray, but Jonah does not. The sailors cast lots to determine who is responsible for the tempest, and Jonah is selected. Jonah admits his guilt and invites them to throw him into the sea so the storm will cease. The sailors shrink from such a deed and struggle to bring the ship back to land. Nevertheless, they fail. They then pray that the God who has caused the storm will not hold them guilty for Jonah's destruction, and they throw him overboard. The sea suddenly becomes calm, and the sailors offer a sacrifice to Jonah's God. God has a "great fish" swallow Jonah. Jonah says a prayer of thanksgiving for deliverance from the sea. At God's command the fish vomits him out on land. God again orders Jonah to preach to Nineveh. Jonah goes and proclaims that Nineveh will soon be destroyed. Everyone in Nineveh believes, repents, and begs God for mercy. God relents and spares the city. Jonah becomes angry and reminds God that he fled for fear that God would be merciful to Nineveh. God provides Jonah with a plant for shade but then destroys the plant. In response to Jonah's anger over the plant's destruction, God says that if Jonah is concerned about a mere plant, he should have pity on the great city of Nineveh.

Jonah appears to be simply a piece of literature without any real historical foundation. To be sure, there apparently was a historical prophet named "Jonah" (2 Kings 14:25), but the historical Jonah predicted Israel's territorial expansion, not the destruction of Nineveh. In fact, the book of Jonah with its "great fish" swallowing a man and three days later vomiting him up on land is basically a fairy tale.

The profound message of the tale is that Pagans sometimes behave better than God's followers, and God's followers should reach out to them. The book of Jonah idealizes the Pagan characters who act far better than Jonah does. During the storm the sailors pray, whereas Jonah does not. Jonah runs away when he first hears God's summons; in response to God's summons the people of Nineveh immediately turn to him. The book also stresses that God has compassion on Pagans and suggests that Israel has a mission to announce God's will to them. Nineveh may be notoriously wicked, but God cares about it and commands Jonah to go there and preach. Consequently, the book looks forward to the universalism of Christianity. The church has a mission to the entire world, including the most notorious parts of it. The church should also have the humility to realize that many people who do not believe in God or Jesus sometimes behave far better than some Christians do. Nevertheless, even these virtuous persons can benefit from learning about the love that God reveals through Jesus.

7

✝

Biblical Wisdom, especially Job; Is God Just?

The ancient Israelites searched for "wisdom," and much of what they found became part of the Old Testament. We may define biblical "wisdom" as reflections on how to think and act in order to have a successful life. Such advice was especially for rulers, junior officials, and children. Wisdom experts collected and formulated their counsels and produced books. Ultimately, a number of these became part of the Bible.

The "wise" based their advice on moral values and lived experience. On the basis of faith, the wise asserted that ethical behavior leads to the blessings of this life: prestige, prosperity, longevity, and a blessed memory. The wise also looked at what actually occurred in people's lives and gave incisive summaries of what they discovered.

We may classify the wisdom writings in the Bible as orthodox or heterodox. The orthodox books, such as Proverbs, make the optimistic assertion that virtue leads to worldly success. Basically Proverbs is a series of adages that monotonously assure us that those who listen to its advice and persevere in virtue will have riches, social respect, good health, and so forth. Of course, this optimistic view supports God's commandments as found elsewhere in the Bible. We should obey God's word, because if we do so we will have tangible benefits. By contrast, the heterodox writings, especially Ecclesiastes, make the contrasting case that in practice there is no correlation between virtue and success, that as often as not the righteous suffer and the wicked prosper. Ecclesiastes is a meditation on the ultimate futility of human existence. The book claims that chance decides most things, and, therefore, even if we do what is right, there is no guarantee that we will end up better off. In any case, death will obliterate everything we have, including all memory of us. Of course, this pessimistic evaluation implicitly raises questions about the desirability of obeying God.

The theological and literary masterpiece of wisdom literature in the Old Testament is the book of Job, because it manages to affirm both the optimism of Proverbs and the pessimism of Ecclesiastes by taking the discussion to a deeper level. Job insists that indeed there is a reward for virtue, but it is not necessarily tangible.

Theologically, the book focuses on two fundamental questions. First, can we treat victims humanely if we hold that virtue leads to success and sin to failure? Second, can we continue to believe that God is good if we admit that sometimes there in an inverse correlation between virtue and success?

We may summarize Job as follows: In the period of the Patriarchs, there lives a supremely righteous man named Job. Satan prompts God to let him test Job with great suffering to see if Job is sincerely devoted to God or is righteous merely from self-interest. We may note that the Old Testament pictures Satan (Hebrew for *adversary*) as something like the prosecuting attorney in heaven. Only in the New Testament is he the Devil. Job loses his property and family and begins to suffer from a painful disease. Initially, Job refuses to blame God. Three friends arrive to comfort him. A long conversation follows. Job curses the day of his birth. His friends respond by arguing that Job's suffering cannot be wholly undeserved because God does not punish the guiltless. They urge Job to repent. Job insists that he is innocent (which the reader knows to be the case). The dialog becomes increasingly acrimonious as the friends insist on Job's guilt and he maintains his innocence. Job's friends, using the logic of orthodox wisdom, claim that he has sinned grievously and, indeed, that he is suffering less than he deserves. God could not be in the wrong. Job responds that his friends are treacherous. Even if he had done wrong, their responsibility is to comfort him. Human life is too short and fragile for great suffering to be of any benefit. God should realize how fragile and transitory our lives are and relent. As the debate continues, Job appeals with increasing confidence to God to demonstrate that he is in the right. Initially Job longs to have an "umpire" so he could speak to God on some basis of equality and question God's fairness. Then Job tells his friends that God is angry with them for using lies to defend him and that God himself would vindicate Job. Finally, Job declares that in real life the evil prosper and the righteous do not. He is utterly innocent and has himself never failed to help those who were suffering. Then God speaks and asks Job a long series of questions. Does Job know all the mysteries of the universe that God created? Was Job present when the world was made? Does he understand the ultimate foundations of reality or the secrets of nature? These questions demonstrate Job's ignorance and show that someone who knows so little is in no position to find fault with God by claiming that God is unjust. Job repents, stating that now that he has actually seen God, he has nothing to say. God then declares that Job's friends have spoken falsely, unlike Job, and that Job must pray for them. Job does so. God restores Job to health and prosperity, and he ends up even better off than he was before Satan afflicted him.

Taken as a whole, the book seems to affirm the following: Innocent people really do suffer unjustly. Therefore, it is cruel and sinful to assume that sufferers must have sinned. Instead, we should do all that we can to help others who are in great need, as Job stresses that he has always done. Nevertheless, God himself is not arbitrary or unjust. We simply do not know enough to criticize God. When we charge that God is not doing what is right, we are implicitly claiming that we could have created a better universe than he has or could run the present one better than he does. Such a claim is obviously ridiculous and arrogant. Not only do we lack the power to make or run a better universe, we lack the power to make or run any universe. Consequently, it is a mistake even in the midst of great, undeserved suffering to blame God. Somehow if we are suffering and keep seeking God, we will meet him, and when we do, we will recognize his goodness. Accordingly, we must not give in to cynicism but, despite suffering, must continue to obey God and trust him and search for him.

As we will see, these perspectives take on additional dimensions in Christian thought in light of the crucifixion of Jesus. The crucifixion certainly demonstrates that in this fallen world, virtue can lead to torture and death. Nevertheless, the crucifixion also demonstrates the unimaginable goodness of a God who suffers for a world that punishes virtue. The crucifixion also shows how our own virtuous suffering can lead us to God. God suffered for doing what was right, and when we do the same, we become more like him and can relate to him more deeply.

Of course, the resurrection of Jesus necessitates a much broader perspective on whether God ultimately rewards the righteous and whether the reward is worth the sacrifice. The resurrection reveals that our earthly lives are only a brief preparation for an eternal existence with God. Job complained that human life is too short to justify the suffering that some people must endure. To this a Christian would follow the lead of St. Paul and claim the opposite: "The sufferings of this present time are not worth comparing to the glory that shall be revealed to us" (Rom. 8:18).

From a modern perspective the most pressing question that the book of Job raises is whether we can still believe that there is a God in view of the horrors that we have recently experienced. When Job was written, few doubted that God (or the gods) existed. The issue was whether God was just. Today atheism is more prevalent, and the strongest argument in its favor is the haunting question of why God does not intervene to end colossal suffering. This question has become all the more pressing in light of the unparalleled slaughters of modern times, including the Holocaust in Germany, the Great Purges in the Soviet Union, the Cultural Revolution in China, and the Killing Fields in Cambodia.

When we deal in detail with Jesus' crucifixion, we will return to the difficult question of why God does not intervene to end the horrors of this life.

8

Israel from the Exile until Jesus; Life after Death in Christian Tradition

In the sixth century B.C.E., the Babylonians took leading Jews into exile. The Babylonians captured Jerusalem in 597 and recaptured it in 586. On both occasions they rounded up Jews who were prominent and took them off to serve in Babylon and other places in the empire.

During the Exile Jewish priests began a new codification of the law. Very probably there had not previously existed a single legal code. Instead, there were different bodies of law. Some existed in writing. Others were oral, consisting of customs that were followed in practice but had never been formally recorded. The Jewish community assumed that the exile was a punishment from God for not following his wishes. As a result, people were anxious to ascertain exactly what God required so that they could do it and he would restore their fortunes.

The law claimed to go back to the time of Moses but was in fact an expansion of earlier principles, some of which may conceivably go back to Moses. The relationship of the biblical law (and subsequent commentaries on it) to the insights of the historical Moses is analogous to the relationship of American constitutional law to the constitution of the United States. The constitution guarantees freedom of speech; constitutional law must struggle with the details, such as whether there is a constitutional right to send pornography over the Internet. Because the law was in some sense an application of Mosaic principles, it was attributed to him and placed in the opening books of the Bible, all of which were written or at least edited during the Exile and subsequently.

This revised law had special characteristics that ultimately guaranteed the survival of the Jewish people. The Mosaic Law combined ethical and ethnic regulations. The ethical regulations mandated high standards, and these caused the Jews to keep a stricter morality than their neighbors. This superior conduct contributed both to Jewish self-respect and to their esteem among Gentiles. The law also mandated an ethnic lifestyle, including what Jews ate, how they dressed, and what holidays they kept. Hence, the law made the Jews visibly different and helped preserve their national identity, especially after they lost both their political independence and ancient homeland.

With the Exile, we begin to get monotheism in the strict sense. Earlier most Israelites had worshiped a variety of gods and goddesses in addition to Yahweh. Even the conservative minority who loyally insisted on the exclusive worship of Yahweh were not monotheists intellectually. To be sure, they believed that he was the most powerful God and had made a special covenant with Israel. Nevertheless, even conservative Jews probably acknowledged that in fact there were other deities. Now due to the Exile Jews were living in the lands of other gods. The exclusive worship of Yahweh could only continue if people believed that other gods did not exist, and we begin to get the polemical insistence that the gods that others worship are mere nothings.

Even though philosophical monotheism arose partly as a result of contingent historical conditions, it expresses profound truth and, as a result, has survived. If there are many gods, we must somehow attempt to placate them all. Consequently, our religious devotion and our everyday lives become fragmented. Monotheism, by contrast, allows us to devote our entire attention to pleasing the only God and, as a result, our lives become focused. Moreover, Christian experience has always been that as our spiritual discernment deepens we discover that only God is unlimited and eternal. Many other spiritual forces exist, but all of them are finite.

We may now briefly summarize the history of the Israelites from the end of the Exile until the time of Jesus. In 539 the Persian Empire conquered Babylon and allowed the exiled Jewish leaders to go home. The Jews then lived in Palestine as an ethnic community under foreign rule. Around 330 B.C.E. the Greeks conquered the Persian Empire, and the Jews came under their rule. In the years 167–164, the insane Greek ruler Antiochus Epiphanes attempted to unify his empire by violently suppressing Judaism. The Jews under the leadership of a priestly family named the Maccabees revolted, and for a century Israel was again politically independent. In 63 B.C.E. the Romans conquered Jerusalem, and Palestine came under Roman domination.

A major theological development in the Greek period was the rise of belief in meaningful life after death. Prior to the third century B.C.E., the Jews did not believe in personal survival after death. Unlike Greek thought which held that the soul and the body were separable, traditional Jewish thought held that the body and soul form a unity. Hence, when the body decays, the spirit does as well, and after death people's consciousness becomes dim. Beginning in the third century B.C.E. a few Jews, probably under the influence of Greek thought, began to believe that at death the soul leaves the body and goes to another realm. In response to martyrdoms during the persecution under Antiochus Epiphanes, perhaps the majority of Jews began to believe in the physical resurrection of the dead at the end of time. At the resurrection God would reassemble our bodies, judge the world, and reward the righteous and punish the wicked. As N. T. Wright has shown, many Jews combined these beliefs, holding that at an individual's demise the soul goes temporarily to another realm and then at the last day rejoins the body when God physically raises it from the dead.[1] Jesus himself apparently held this composite view, since we have sayings from him that mention both risen souls (e.g., Luke 16:19–31) and a future physical resurrection (e.g., Luke 20:27–38).

Apocalypticism appeared along with faith in the resurrection. Apocalypticism is the belief that God will bring the universe as we know it to a cataclysmic end and then produce a new and better world. Like biblical prophecy, apocalypticism looks into the heart of God and attempts to evaluate the present from his point of view. And like prophecy, apocalypticism predicts the future on the basis of how God intends to respond. What distinguishes apocalypticism from prophecy is that prophecy looks forward to God acting within history, whereas apocalypticism pictures the end of history at least as it has always been. Earlier, biblical prophecy predicted things that normally occur, such as defeat or victory in war, famine or an abundant harvest, and so forth. By contrast, apocalypticism predicts the destruction of present reality and the advent of a new heaven and earth. Apocalypticism often arises in a situation when the oppressed are so helpless that redemption within history lacks credibility. In the case of the Old Testament, the persecution of Antiochus Epiphanes especially stimulated the belief that soon God would intervene and physically raise the Jewish martyrs from the grave. The book of Daniel is the first book in the Bible to predict the resurrection of the dead and was a direct response to the persecution.

Apocalypticism later furnished the context within which the first followers of Jesus interpreted his unexpected resurrection. As we shall see, after the death of Jesus his followers discovered that his tomb had become empty and then met Jesus risen from the dead. Since Jesus had risen from the dead, the first Christians concluded that the general resurrection foretold by the apocalypticists was imminent. They began to preach that Jesus was about to return and judge the world.

As a result of subsequent historical experience, the church increasingly emphasized the departure of the soul but still retained faith in an eventual physical resurrection. Of course, the world did not end. Increasingly, Christian teaching stressed that the soul leaves the body at death and goes to heaven or hell. Nevertheless, the church honored its apocalyptic heritage by still awaiting the ultimate return of Christ from heaven and some final physical resurrection in which the soul would be reunited with the body.

As a contemporary Christian, I would affirm the view that at death the soul goes to God for judgment. This view not only accords with traditional doctrine but now also seems to be substantiated by contemporary near-death experiences. Thanks to modern medicine, it is now possible to revive many people after their hearts have stopped beating. Such people frequently report that they leave their bodies, go through a tunnel, and encounter a being of light. This being walks them through the events of their lives and invites them to evaluate how they have lived.

I would also hold that God has a plan for history and that history will reach some intended climax. We do not know the details. Perhaps apocalyptic is too pessimistic about the present world. Maybe God will not have to produce a new earth because we have destroyed the present one. What is certain is that a loving God intends for history to reach a glorious destiny, and we should remain confident that in due course he will somehow bring it to pass.

NOTES

1. N. T. Wright, *The Resurrection of the Son of God* (Minneapolis, MN: Fortress, 2003), 156–206.

9

✢

A Sketch of Jesus' Life and Personality

Our information about the life of Jesus comes almost entirely from four brief biographies with the titles "Matthew," "Mark," "Luke," and "John" from the traditional names of the authors. These books were written toward the end of the first century and are in Greek. We normally call them "gospels," from the Greek word for "good news," and they are the opening books in the New Testament. We must depend almost solely on them to learn about Jesus, because the other ancient documents that describe him appeared much later and seem unreliable.[1]

There are some historical problems with the gospels as sources for information about Jesus. No one was video taping Jesus when he was alive, and presumably even from the first, people did not recall exactly, but only basically, what Jesus said or did. The gospels were written down decades after the death of Jesus. The earliest, Mark, did not appear until around the year 70. By that time the authentic memories about Jesus had mixed with material expressing the convictions of the early church and with legends. In addition, the evangelists wrote the gospels to address specific problems of their own time and shaped the words and deeds of Jesus to do so.

Nevertheless, the gospels give us the thrust of Jesus' life and teaching. The four gospels were all written within seventy years of Jesus' death. At least a few eyewitnesses were still alive even when the evangelists were at work. Such people must have been prominent in the church, because the very fact that they had known Jesus gave them prestige. For them Jesus' words and deed were especially memorable. These witnesses would have helped keep the tradition from becoming hopelessly distorted. The picture of the social life that the gospels provide coheres basically with what we learn from other sources about the environment of Jesus. The gospels contain information that was embarrassing to the church. Even in the latest and least historically accurate of the gospels, John, we still read that Jesus' family did not believe in him (John 7:5), that his closest disciples denied or betrayed him (e.g., 13:21–30, 18:15–18), that his enemies accused him of being insane or demon possessed (e.g., 10:20), and that at least on occasion Jesus himself suffered from anxiety and hesitation (e.g., 12:27). The followers of Jesus would never have invented such material, and the presence of such undeniably authentic memories suggests that much of the positive material about Jesus must be accurate too. Consequently, most of what is in the gospels is at least either a reasonable summary of what Jesus said and did or a reasonable interpretation of its significance.

We can now sketch Jesus' life. Jesus was born into a lower class Jewish family. During the early first century, he grew up in Nazareth, a village in Galilee. His childhood is obscure, and there is no reason to assume that outwardly it differed greatly from that of his neighbors. He subsequently did not choose to get married, and it is worth noting that there was some tradition of religious celibacy at the time. When Jesus was a young adult, John the Baptist was engaging in his public ministry. John was a prophet who preached in the wilderness of Judea. His message was that God would soon judge the Jews through the coming Messiah ("Christ" in Greek), and only those who repented would be saved. John was apparently especially critical of the leaders of Jewish society. As a sign of repentance, he administered baptism (a ritual bath we discuss later). Jesus journeyed south and received baptism at John's hands and may have been John's disciple for a period. When John was arrested and executed, Jesus returned to Galilee. There he traveled about preaching and accepting hospitality and financial support from sympathizers. In contrast to John, he adopted a more worldly lifestyle. He attended banquets and associated freely with "sinners" (e.g., Matt. 11:16–19). He had little concern for purity regulations and sometimes violated the mandatory Sabbath rest, especially when responding to human need. He drove out "demons" and healed the sick (the miracles are discussed later on pages 65–71). He attracted followers and named an inner circle of twelve who apparently symbolized the new Israel that Jesus was calling into being. His followers pressed him to declare himself king, but he resisted. Meanwhile, his unconventional behavior shocked pious people. Toward what was to be the end of his life, he went to the capital Jerusalem to confront the nation with his message. There he staged a demonstration in the temple to symbolize that it was to be destroyed and replaced by his kingdom. The Romans executed him as a revolutionary. Jesus was only in his thirties.

We can also sketch Jesus' personality. Jesus loved the pleasures of life but was not attached to them. According to the gospels, Jesus often attended dinner parties, and some of the stories that he himself told feature banquets. Apparently he loved good food and wine. His enemies even accused him of being a glutton and a drunk (Matt. 11:19). Nevertheless, it is clear that he was not attached to the pleasures of life. He lived as an itinerant, and he traveled light. Indeed, he taught his followers to take virtually nothing on their journeys but to rely on the hospitality of the villages to which they were going. He also knew that sometimes he and his followers would not receive hospitality. He told his followers that if a village would not give them lodging, they would have to go on to the next. Ultimately, he journeyed to Jerusalem and accepted his death by torture as God's call for him. Jesus lived one day at a time in trust (Matt. 6:25–34). Of course, an itinerant has to live this way.

Jesus was compassionate toward people in need. He felt their physical and emotional suffering. He acted to eliminate their pain. Sometimes he worked miracles to help the sick and the hungry. He gave the despised inclusion. We read in the gospels that he often touched rejected people or took them into his arms. He was notorious for associating with "sinners."

A striking characteristic of Jesus was that he could see into people's hearts and respond to the real person, and, consequently, he brought people's true selves to light. In story after story we read that Jesus discerned hidden agendas. People would try to trick him somehow. But Jesus would read their minds and expose the plots.

Jesus was impatient with all forms of pride and hypocrisy, especially among "religious" people. He attacked both his critics and even his own disciples for "play acting," for pretending to be more righteous than they were, and for twisting religious law for their own selfish advantage.

He could not be manipulated either by individuals or social regulations. People repeatedly tried to trap him, to force him to say something he did not wish to say or do something he did not wish to do. They always failed. Jesus had a sovereign freedom.

Jesus acted with authority. He seldom appealed to custom or scripture or even God to verify what he claimed. Instead, he simply stated what he knew to be true. He also did whatever he felt called to do, even when this obedience involved violating custom or law. Indeed, in the famous Sermon on the Mount in Matthew's Gospel, there is a section in which Jesus pointedly contrasts what his audience has heard from tradition with what Jesus is saying to them now. Strikingly, Jesus does not back up his own views but merely states them (Matt. 5:21–48).

He was humble and pointed away from himself to God. Jesus was reticent to accept any praise for himself but stressed the greatness of his Heavenly Father. He taught that it was pardonable to slander him but not to slander God's Spirit (Luke 12:10). He refused even to be called "good" and insisted that only God was good (Mark 10:18). He proclaimed the coming of God's rule, not his own.

All the above came from his relationship to God, which was characterized by intimacy and obedience. Jesus' love of life, his compassion, his sovereign freedom, and the other characteristics mentioned above seem to have been fruits of his special closeness to the divine. He called God his "Father," and in doing so seemed to imply that his own relationship to God differed from that of other people. All Jesus' striking characteristics proceeded from that relationship. Jesus loved life, because life was God's gift to him; Jesus' compassion was an expression of God's compassion; Jesus could not be manipulated, because God cannot be manipulated. Jesus felt that he knew directly what God wanted, and Jesus placed his Father's will above all other considerations. Ultimately, Jesus even accepted crucifixion, because he discerned that this horrific death was his Father's will for him.

NOTES

1. Some scholars hold that the Gospel of Thomas is also an important source of information about Jesus. I believe that a number of the sayings in Thomas do go back to Jesus. Nevertheless, Thomas is of limited value, because it tells us nothing about the life of Jesus, only what he said. Like many scholars I believe that Thomas is a second century document and, therefore, significantly later (and less reliable) than the New Testament gospels.

10

The Birth of Jesus and the Doctrine of the Incarnation

In the gospels we have three different treatments of the birth (and early infancy) of Jesus. In Matthew's account, a man named Joseph, who is a descendant of King David, is engaged to a woman named Mary. While Mary is still a virgin, she becomes pregnant by the power of God's Spirit. An angel appears to Joseph in a dream and tells him not to break off the engagement and that the future child will be the savior. Jesus is born at Bethlehem. Mysterious astrologers (Magi) appear at Jerusalem and announce that a star has foretold the birth of a Jewish king. The reigning Jewish ruler, Herod the Great, becomes alarmed and sends the Magi to locate the child. The Magi follow the star to the house of Mary and Joseph and present gifts. An angel appears to Joseph in a dream and tells him to take his family and flee to Egypt, and Joseph obeys. Herod then slaughters the male infants of Bethlehem in a vain effort to kill the foretold king. After the death of Herod, Joseph with Mary and Jesus returns to Palestine from Egypt, and they settle in Nazareth.

Luke tells the story differently. In Nazareth the angel Gabriel appears to Mary when she is still a virgin and is engaged to Joseph. The angel announces that Mary will bear a child by the power of the Holy Spirit. The child will be called the "Son of God" and found an everlasting kingdom, and in response Mary praises God. The Roman emperor decrees that everyone must register. Joseph, who is descended from King David, goes to his ancestral home of

Bethlehem to register and takes along Mary. When they arrive, there are no accommodations, and Mary gives birth and places Jesus in a manger. Meanwhile, an angel appears to nearby shepherds and announces the birth of the Messiah. The shepherds come and find Mary, Joseph, and the baby Jesus. The family remains in Jerusalem for the ceremonies of circumcision and purification and then returns to Nazareth where Jesus will grow up.

John's Gospel gives a more theological account of Jesus' entry into the world. According to John, an eternal "Word" dwelt with God "in the beginning" and shared in divinity. Through this Word God created the universe. This Word then "became flesh," that is, was born as a human being.

These three accounts obviously disagree on most details. We may note, for example, that Matthew tacitly assumes that Mary and Joseph originally lived in Bethlehem and only because of the murderous plot of Herod had to leave, ultimately ending up in Nazareth. By contrast, Luke tacitly assumes that Mary and Joseph originally lived in Nazareth and only temporarily visited Bethlehem so that Joseph could register.

It appears that the accounts of the birth of Jesus are based on a mixture of history, prophecy, and theology. Part of the accounts is historical. Jesus certainly grew up in Nazareth. His mother was named Mary, and his (step) father was named Joseph.

Part of the accounts clearly fulfills biblical prophecy. Among these are Jesus' descent from King David, his conception by a virgin, and his birth at Bethlehem. In each case, the gospels provide us with a "prophecy" from the Old Testament. Thus, in connection with Jesus' birth at Bethlehem, Matthew explicitly quotes Micah 5:2, which states that a ruler of Israel will come from Bethlehem. It is difficult to know whether such details are historical. On the one hand, these details could have been recalled precisely because they fulfilled Old Testament texts. On the other hand, the evangelists (and earlier Christians) could have begun with the faith that Jesus must have fulfilled such prophecies and then proceeded to imagine that he did. Or a conservative could claim that God actually did reveal to ancient prophets what would occur centuries later at the birth of Jesus. Other details, such as John's claim that Jesus was God incarnate, clearly reflect theological convictions that arose later.

In any case, the primary message of all three accounts of Jesus' birth is basically the same: Through Jesus, God himself has come into our midst in a new and more intimate way. Matthew tells us that Jesus is "Emmanuel" and reminds us that in Hebrew "Emmanuel" means "God with us" (Matt. 1:23). Luke tells us that Jesus was conceived by the Holy Spirit and is the Son of God (Luke 1:35). John insists that through Jesus, the Eternal Word who is God has become "flesh and dwelt and among us" (John 1:1, 14).

Historically, belief in the incarnation—God becoming human—resulted from the resurrection. After Jesus' death, his disciples had experiences that convinced them that he had risen from the dead and now exercised the authority that belongs to God alone. We discuss the resurrection in detail later. For the time being, we may note that belief in the incarnation inevitably followed from the conclusion that the risen Jesus was divine. A person cannot become God. Hence, if the risen Christ was God, Jesus must always have been divine. The only explanation for this astounding fact was that God himself had chosen to be born as a human being. Already in his letter to the Philippians, written around the year 60, Paul insists that prior to his incarnation Jesus existed in the "form of God" and then "emptied himself" and "was born in the likeness of human beings" (Phil. 2:6–7).

Within subsequent Christian thought, the incarnation was central. Of course, the life and teaching of Jesus continued to inspire the faithful. However, it was the extraordinary claim that, through Jesus, God himself had become a human being, shared our common life, and, like all human beings, suffered death that became the most important and distinctive claim of Christianity. Thus, the primary official statement of Christian faith, the Nicene Creed, says nothing about what Jesus taught. Instead, the creed stresses that Jesus Christ is "the only Son of God, eternally begotten of the Father, God from God" and then "came down from heaven" and "became incarnate" and "suffered death."

Unfortunately, the Greek philosophic framework within which traditional theology operated made the incarnation seem impossible. Classical Greek philosophy insisted that God cannot change or suffer. God is, by definition, perfect, and something that is perfect cannot change. If it did change, it would have to go from perfection to imperfection. Similarly, God cannot suffer because suffering is a defect. Of course, the doctrine of the incarnation necessarily implies that God did change and suffer: He took on a human life and ultimately experienced crucifixion. Hence, classical theologians had the impossible task of explaining how God could become human without changing and could be crucified without suffering.

Contemporary theology provides a more helpful framework that makes the incarnation logically conceivable. Today we can see that what makes something "perfect" depends on the thing in question. A perfect geometric concept does not change, but a perfect human being surely does. The ability to change and suffer is part of God's perfection, since "God is love" (1 John 4:8, 16). When we love someone, we always change, because they become part of us, and we suffer if they suffer.

As Donald Gelpi points out, the incarnation occurred when God assumed the autonomy of a human life and thereby experienced human life firsthand.[1] God knows and experiences every human life completely. However, he experiences our lives secondhand. If I am in pain, he experiences it as my pain. A mother whose child is afraid of the dark feels the child's fear, but the mother herself is not afraid of the dark. In the incarnation God took on a human life as his own life. Hence, he experienced limitation and suffering directly.

We can also see how the incarnation brings salvation. By sharing a human experience, God could reveal to us who he is and what a human being can become through union with him. God could also share the vulnerability and pain of human existence firsthand and, thereby, have a deeper basis for relating to us. The knowledge that God suffered in the same way that we suffer gives us a deeper basis for relating to him too. We return to these reflections when we deal with the crucifixion.

NOTES

1. Donald L. Gelpi, S.J., *The Firstborn of Many: A Christology for Converting Christians* (3 vols.; Milwaukee, WI: Marquette University Press, 2001), III:225–354.

11

✢

The Baptism of Jesus and Baptism in Church History

Ceremonies are important. They especially help us make transitions. Thus, we use ceremonies to celebrate the great events in life such as birth, becoming an adult, retirement, and death. We also use ceremonies to make fundamental commitments between individuals and groups. We perform marriages, sign contracts, make treaties. Indeed, it is hard to imagine human existence without ceremonies.

In general a ceremony produces what it symbolizes. The exchange of marriage vows actually changes the relationship between the two parties and makes them husband and wife. The signing of a treaty actually changes the relationship between two nations and makes peace. Of course, if a ceremony is hypocritical, it does not produce what it purportedly signifies. If a nation signs a peace treaty and then invades, the treaty does not make peace. Nevertheless, it still produces what it actually signified. The aggressor nation used the treaty as a means of betrayal, and the aggrieved nation naturally feels betrayed.

A "sacrament" is a ceremony that changes or reaffirms a sacred relationship, and historically, Christianity has had many sacraments. Thus, ordination is a sacrament, since it installs people to lead the church in God's name and gives them special sacred duties and powers. Similarly, marriage is a sacrament since it confers

God's blessing on a couple and thereby makes their relationship sacred. Penance is a sacrament, since it restores a sinner's relationship to God by formally declaring God's forgiveness after the sinner has made a confession. Unction, anointing the sick with blessed oil, is a sacrament, because the ceremony reaffirms God's love and confers his healing power when a person is in special need.

Nevertheless, two sacraments have been especially central: baptism and Eucharist. One sign of their centrality is that the church has always expected every member to get baptized and receive the Eucharist. The other sacraments are only for some people, as in the case of ordination and marriage, or are only for some situations, as the in the case of penance and unction. Moreover, only baptism and Eucharist indisputably have their authorization in Jesus' commandments as found in the gospels. For example, in Matthew 28:19 Jesus commands his disciples to baptize all nations, and in Luke 22:19 he instructs them to repeat the Eucharist in his memory.

"Baptism" is a ceremonial washing. The word comes from Greek and literally means to immerse or wash.

Historically, baptism originated with John who consequently came to have the nickname "the Baptist." John preached that God was about to judge Israel through the coming messiah and the nation had to prepare. John administered baptism as a sign of national repentance. Those who received the ceremonial bath acknowledged the sins of society and their complicity in them and made a commitment to live righteously.

Jesus received baptism just prior to the beginning of his career as a religious teacher, and the ceremony seems to have been a turning point in his life. Previously Jesus had lived in Galilee and apparently not engaged in any public ministry. He then left his home, journeyed to Judea, and received baptism at John's hands. The gospels tell us that at his baptism, Jesus had a vision of God's Spirit coming into him and a heavenly voice declaring that he was God's "beloved Son" (e.g., Matt. 3:16–17). While this scene reflects subsequent Christian theology, there is every reason to assume that Jesus' baptism was a transforming event. By sacramentally acknowledging that his nation was deeply involved in sin and by pledging to live a righteous life, Jesus implicitly made a commitment to begin his own mission to God's people. It appears that immediately thereafter Jesus himself baptized people (John 3:22).

Nevertheless, soon Jesus stopped baptizing. The ruler Herod Antipas had John arrested and executed. Jesus must have been devastated, and the gospels tell us he engaged in a long fast and retreated to his native Galilee. Subsequently, he apparently did not administer baptism, since the gospels never mention Jesus performing the ceremony during the remainder of his ministry.

Jesus stopped baptizing probably because he thought that the kingdom, whose coming John had proclaimed, was now arriving. John's baptism had been to prepare people for the coming reign of God and its Messiah. Now Jesus concluded that in his own ministry, God's reign was beginning, and that in some sense he was the Messiah ("Christ" in Greek).

After Jesus' death and resurrection (discussed later), the early church revived baptism and used it as a ceremony to mark becoming a Christian. In the church baptism no longer was a preparation for the coming of the Messiah. Instead, it was now the mark that an individual accepted Jesus as the Messiah and was joining the community of those who worshiped him as Lord.

As an initiation rite into the church, baptism sacramentally conferred the blessings of Christian life. Baptism conferred the forgiveness of previous sins. Entering the church signaled a break with one's prior moral and spiritual life and the intent to be righteous subsequently. God honored that intent by pardoning the past. Baptism also conferred the Holy Spirit. John the Baptist had foretold that the Messiah would baptize with the Spirit. After the resurrection of Jesus, the church experienced the presence of the Spirit in the community. By joining that community, new members opened themselves to receiving the same Spirit. Particularly in the first century, baptism symbolized that within the church there were supposed to be no social divisions. Every Christian received baptism, and this commonality underlined that in Jesus all were one. As St. Paul wrote, among the baptized, "There is no Jew or Greek; there is no slave or free; there is no male and female" (Gal. 3:28). Symbolically, baptism also involved participation in Jesus' death and resurrection. By going down into the water, a believer "died" to the old life, and by coming up out of the water rose to a new one in Christ. An implication was that baptism began one's eternal life.

Very quickly it became standard to baptize people in the name of the Father and the Son and the Holy Spirit. It appears that in the earliest church, baptism was done in the name of Jesus, since the Acts of the Apostles repeatedly states this (e.g., Acts 2:38). Soon, however, the church took literally Jesus' command at the end of Matthew's Gospel and began to baptize people in the name of the three persons of the Trinity.

Because the church was an organic community rather than a collection of individuals, the early church administered baptism to children of Christian families. Often whole families converted to Christianity, and the children received baptism along with the adults. In Christianity baptism replaced the Jewish rite of male circumcision. Jewish boys received circumcision on the eighth day of their lives to mark their entrance into God's people. Therefore, it seemed natural to baptize infants from Christian families shortly after birth.

To help explain why infants needed a sacrament bestowing "forgiveness," the church developed the doctrine of original sin (see earlier discussion). We all participate in the primordial sin of Adam and need to be cleansed from it.

Especially with the rise of individualism in modern times, both original sin and infant baptism have become controversial. Individualists insist that sin can only result from our personal choices and that someone can only enter the church by making an individual decision. On this logic, people should not receive baptism until they have reached "the age of reason." As a result, some Christian groups, including the "Baptists," do not baptize young children. More traditional Christians have continued the ancient practice.

Nevertheless, the difference between the denominations over baptism is often not as great as it might seem. In practice, some denominations who do not baptize infants have them blessed or dedicated. The blessing or dedication symbolically welcomes babies into the community and sacramentally places them under God's protection and thus accomplishes much that infant baptism does. In practice, some denominations who baptize infants insist that when the children reach the age of reason, they must go through another sacrament called confirmation. At confirmation people make a public declaration of their faith in God and their commitment to the Christian life and receive a solemn blessing. Hence, in practice many denominations who baptize infants and many who do not both recognize that children of Christian families are members of the community but also later need to make an adult commitment.

Another controversial issue is whether baptism must be by immersion. Historically, baptism was initially by immersion. Nevertheless, since enough water was not always available for immersion, the church soon allowed baptism by pouring water on the head. Of course, pouring water on the head was much easier, especially when baptizing infants or people in poor health, and it became standard in some Christian communities. Other communities (e.g., "Baptists") have insisted on immersion.

Here again, however, the differences are often not great. All Christian communities allow baptism by immersion. Indeed, they would agree that it is preferable in theory, especially since immersion symbolizes more graphically sharing in Jesus' death and resurrection. Most Christian communities who insist on baptism by immersion for their own members accept that baptism by effusion is nevertheless a valid baptism for other Christians.

12

✟

The Teaching of Jesus

The principal theme of Jesus' message was the kingdom of God. The theme pervades his sayings in the gospels. For example, we find it in his model prayer, often called the "Our Father" or the "Lord's Prayer." Jesus taught us to pray, "Your kingdom come." The kingdom is also what the various stories (parables) that Jesus told illustrate.

By the "kingdom," Jesus meant God reigning over a renewed Israel that would transform the world. Like many other Jews of his day, Jesus believed that the world had fallen under the power of evil. Israel had sinned and, as a consequence, God had become distant and was allowing other nations to oppress it. Satan and his demons were loose in the world causing sickness and death. Soon God would intervene to make Israel righteous and restore it to favor. Then through his renewed people God would bring the entire world to know and obey him. Ultimately, God would destroy the power of Satan, raise the dead, judge the world, and renew the creation.

Jesus' fundamental contention was that the kingdom was coming through the movement that he himself was starting. On one occasion he claimed that a miracle he had just worked showed that the kingdom had come (e.g., Luke 11:20). On another occasion, Jesus insisted that he was about to kindle a fire that would consume the world (Luke 12:49). We may especially note that he chose an inner circle of twelve, and these symbolized the twelve tribes of the new and more blessed Israel that he was calling into being.

When Jesus was alive, it did not seem that he and his followers would change the world. Jesus himself appeared to be a minor figure. He came from an obscure background. He lacked religious credentials, since he was neither a priest nor an accredited rabbi. Many came to hear him, but few converted. He had numerous critics. His committed followers shared his lack of status. As fishermen, former prostitutes, tax collectors, and the like, they mostly came from the lower classes, and some had dubious reputations. Consequently, Jesus' claim that he and his disciples were beginning a new Israel that would one day bring God's blessings to the world appeared absurd.

In response to the seeming absurdity of his claims, Jesus stressed that in the present the kingdom was hidden but was active and growing. He compared what he was doing to a woman who placed—actually "hid"—a little yeast in a mound of flour, but in due course it leavened everything (e.g., Matt. 13:33). Or he compared himself and his movement to a mustard seed, which is tiny but grows into a great herb (Matt. 13:31–32). Jesus freely admitted that he and his followers would even suffer setbacks like a farmer who planted wheat and then discovered that weeds were also sprouting (Matt. 13:24–30). Nevertheless, he insisted that in the end, there would be a vast harvest. Some of what he sowed would bear a hundredfold (Matt. 13:23).

To join the movement that Jesus was starting (i.e., "to enter the kingdom" now), one had to realize that the kingdom was supremely valuable and be willing to give up everything else for it. A person had to perceive that the kingdom was nothing less than the definitive intervention of God into history and that those who joined it would both change history and have an eternal reward (e.g., Mark 10:28–30). Then one had to be prepared to renounce anything that might block allegiance to Jesus and his cause. Jesus taught that the kingdom was like a merchant who discovered a pearl of vast worth and sold everything to purchase it (Mat. 13:45–46) and that loyalty to the kingdom must take precedence even over loyalty to one's father and mother (e.g., Luke 14:26).

Jesus claimed that in the present the kingdom was becoming visible in several ways. First, Jesus' miracles revealed the kingdom, since his healings were breaking the power of sickness and death, and his exorcisms were overthrowing the reign of Satan. We deal with the miracles at length in the next chapter.

The new closeness that Jesus' followers had with God also revealed the kingdom. Jesus called God his "Father," and in doing so claimed a unique intimacy with him. Jesus also taught his followers to think of God as their loving and forgiving father. Indeed, the model prayer he gave them began by addressing God as "Father." This closeness to God must have seemed extraordinary in a world that felt that God had temporarily withdrawn his favor.

The reconciliation of God's people, especially the inclusion of people who were socially unacceptable, was another sign of the kingdom. Jesus said that through him, God was gathering the "lost sheep"of his nation and making them part of the new Israel. He converted prostitutes and people who had collected taxes for the hated government and insisted that all his disciples eat together as a family. He taught that when we ask God to forgive our sins, we must forgive anyone who has sinned against us.

An especially visible and radical dimension of the kingdom was Jesus' insistence that his followers must surrender all social privilege and live as equals. He insisted that in his fellowship the first must be as the last, and the last as the first (e.g., Mark 9:35). One consequence was that women became prominent among his committed followers to the scandal of the larger society, which denied females the right to become religious leaders. Another consequence was economic equality. Jesus insisted that it was easier for a camel to go through the eye of a needle than for the rich to be part of his movement. At least those who wanted to join the inner core of his disciples had to give away their wealth (Mark 10:17–27).

The aspect of the kingdom that inspired the most resentment was Jesus' teaching that people must give up hatred for outsiders. Under Roman rule, Jews in Palestine were preserving their cultural identity by teaching their children to despise Gentiles, and some Jews were even planning armed revolt. In response to this polarized atmosphere, Jesus insisted that we must love our enemies and never resort to violence. Jesus probably thought that his followers would overcome their enemies through suffering compassion. In any case, as N. T. Wright has argued, Jesus believed that the rampant nationalism of his time would lead to catastrophe, including the destruction of the temple.[1] Not surprisingly, Jesus' opposition to the extreme "patriotism" of his day inspired widespread resentment and helped lead to his execution (discussed later on pages 82–84).

Finally, Jesus felt that the coming of the kingdom was giving people the power to recognize and overcome hypocrisy. As we noted earlier, Jesus was especially impatient with hypocrisy. In particular, he became angry with people who kept every religious regulation and yet were arrogant and selfish. He apparently felt that hypocrisy is what keeps people from repentance and reform. People who recognize their sins are eager to improve and willing to accept God's help. But people who pretend that they are already righteous never grow. As we have seen, Jesus exposed people's hidden agendas. Underlying this aggressive behavior must have been the conviction that, through his own preaching, people would be able to recognize the hidden evil in the core of their beings and allow God to begin to change it.

In order to expose hypocrisy, Jesus taught in paradoxes. Normally, his sayings would point to a general truth but would be so extreme or vague that they could not be taken literally. He would proclaim things like, "If your hand causes you to sin, cut it off" (Mark 9:43), or, "If you had faith as a grain of mustard seed, you would say to this mulberry tree, 'Be rooted up and planted in the sea,' and it would obey you" (Luke 17:6). Such statements certainly contain a general thrust. We should make every effort to resist sin; even a little trust in God can accomplish great things. But we cannot take them literally; chopping off a hand will not make someone less sinful; a minuscule faith will not uproot trees. By giving general principles and not allowing people to apply them woodenly, Jesus was making it impossible for his audiences to substitute outward conformity to rules for genuine conversion. Instead, his audiences would have to search for the "spirit" of Jesus' teaching and consider what in their own hearts was blocking understanding and following that spirit.

Jesus insisted that in the future the kingdom would suddenly and unexpectedly come in power and expose every heart (Matt. 25:1–30). God would impose his rule on all, but no one could know in advance exactly when. The kingdom would appear as unexpectedly as a thief in the night. Accordingly, the coming would catch Israel unaware. God would publicly reveal everyone's secrets. Everything that was hidden would become visible for all to see.

With the unexpected coming of the kingdom in power, God would reverse our external status and confirm our spiritual one. The powerful and prominent in this world would suffer. The poor and the hungry would be exalted. Those who had made sacrifices to express their love of God or of their neighbors would be rewarded. All who had made sacrifices to enter the kingdom when it was hidden would receive commendation from God and enter more deeply into his glory. By contrast, all who had rejected the kingdom earlier would come to ruin.

Apparently, toward the end of his life, Jesus concluded that Jerusalem would be destroyed before the coming of the kingdom. When Jesus came to the city to confront it with his message, most people rejected him, and, of course, ultimately he suffered crucifixion. In response to this rejection, Jesus, like the prophets of old, predicted disaster. The city and its temple would be destroyed.

It is to be noted, however, that Jesus did not give any detailed description of the future. All that he basically taught was that soon disaster would befall unrepentant Israel and that later God would establish his loving rule over the entire earth. There were few details, and most of what Jesus did say was in metaphors, images that could not be taken literally.

As a Christian I would hold that basically subsequent events fulfilled Jesus' vision. The Jews in Palestine did revolt two generations later, and in the end the Romans destroyed Jerusalem and its temple. Meanwhile, God vindicated Jesus by raising him from the dead (discussed later). Afterwards, his disciples proclaimed his message, and ultimately Christianity became the largest and most influential religion on earth.

Of course, Jesus' comments about the choices we make in the present and their consequences for our future apply equally well to our lives as individuals. In the present each of us must choose whether we are going to pursue externals—wealth, prestige, pleasure, power over others—or whether we are going to focus on God's love and follow the humble self-sacrifice that Jesus advocated. As we make this decision, we should remember that for each of us the end can come at any moment, and must come within the short span of a human life. When that end does come, we lose the externals. All that we have as we face God's judgment or even consider our legacy on earth is the good that we have done. Jesus himself told a parable of a rich man who suddenly died while looking forward to years of self-indulgence (Luke 12:13–21).

As the inaugurator of the kingdom, Jesus thought that he was the long-awaited Messiah, but not the sort of Messiah most people were expecting. His preaching of the coming of the kingdom presupposed that the kingdom would culminate God's plan for Israel and the world and thus fulfill Old Testament prophetic hope. Jesus himself chose the twelve to be the symbolic heads of the new Israel, and by making this choice he implicitly set himself even above them. During his lifetime various people proclaimed Jesus as the Messiah or charged that he was himself making that claim. Jesus never denied the assertion. However, he did not preach that he was the Messiah. Most people thought that the Messiah would be a military conqueror, and Jesus had no such agenda.

Perhaps the best summary of Jesus' teaching is that through him, universal love was becoming possible. In keeping with his Jewish heritage, Jesus insisted that the two primary commandments were to love God and to love one's neighbor (e.g., Mark 12:28–34). However, Jesus radicalized the second commandment by insisting that one's neighbor included everyone, even notorious sinners, even foreigners, even one's enemy. Of course, it is natural to hate one's enemy. Jesus believed that through his messianic mission, God would enable people to love even those whom they naturally hate.

NOTES

1. N. T. Wright, *Jesus and the Victory of God* (Minneapolis, MN: Fortress, 1996), 322–336.

13

✣

The Miracles of Jesus and Their Significance

There is overwhelming historical evidence that Jesus healed the sick and expelled "demons." The miraculous cures appear frequently in the gospels and occur in every layer of the tradition. The miracles appear in the stories about Jesus, in his own sayings, and in the editorial comments of the evangelists. By subsequently attempting to work miracles in the name of Jesus, the early Christians implicitly bore witness to the fact that their founder had performed them. Even ancient non-Christian sources implicitly attest the wonders of Jesus. The nearly contemporary Jewish historian Josephus wrote that Jesus was a worker of "strange deeds," and later the Jewish Talmud accused Jesus of having practiced "sorcery." The earliest written records that Jesus worked miracles (esp., the Gospel of Mark) appeared only around forty years after his death. Hence, on objective historical grounds we have more evidence that Jesus worked miracles than any other fact about him, other than he was crucified.

By contrast, as John P. Meier has argued, with the exception of the feeding of the multitude, Jesus' nature miracles may not be historical.[1] The gospels contain only eight stories in which Jesus changes something in the natural world, as opposed to restoring sick or deceased human beings. With the exception of Jesus feeding thousands of people with a few loaves of bread, the nature miracles are not well attested. The majority of these stories appear in only one source. For example, only in John's Gospel do we read that Jesus once changed water into wine (John 2:1–11). To be sure some of the nature miracles are in Matthew and/or Luke as well as Mark, but, since Matthew and Luke used Mark as part of their bibliography, we still have only one ultimate source. The nature miracles often do not cohere with what Jesus otherwise did. The cursing of the fig tree (Matt. 21:18–19; Mark 11:12–14, 20) is the only curse miracle in the gospels and does not easily fit with Jesus' message of forgiveness and mercy. Similarly, the walking on water is the only miracle that Jesus seems to work simply for his own convenience (Matt. 14:22–33, Mark 6:45–52, John 6:15–21). The stories of the nature miracles may have arisen in the early church to help express the faith that Jesus was divine. Jesus used fictional stories to convey his thoughts, and the early church may have used imaginary stories about him to express its own convictions about who he was.

According to Mark's Gospel, Jesus sometimes had difficulty performing his healings and exorcisms, and this difficulty must be historical. In chapter 8 we read that Jesus has to try twice to heal a blind man. The first time that Jesus lays hands on him, the man gains only partial sight and cannot distinguish people from trees. Only on the second try does Jesus succeed in restoring sight completely (Mark 8:22–26). In chapter 9 when Jesus first lays his hands on a demon-possessed (epileptic?) boy, the child falls to the ground and seems to be dead. Only when Jesus lays his hands on the boy a second time is the child all right (Mark 9:14–29). Since Mark was a Christian writing for Christians, he could scarcely have made up such an embarrassment, nor could the earlier Christian tradition on which Mark drew. Consequently, on occasion Jesus must have had problems performing his miracles.

Jesus' ability to work miracles was primarily responsible for making him a public figure. Jesus' preaching alone would not have made him prominent. As we saw above, his central claim was that God was beginning a new era of history through his own ministry. Given Jesus' lack of credentials and minuscule following, that claim by itself would have seemed implausible. It was Jesus' healings and exorcisms that gave his message what credibility it had. Consequently, Jesus himself sometimes pointed to his miracles to verify his overall message. Thus, when John the Baptist sent word asking him if he was the prophesied Messiah, Jesus told the messengers to report his healings (Matt. 11:2–6).

As Meier has emphasized, Jesus' miracles differed in important respects from the reputed deeds of ancient magicians.[2] In the gospels Jesus often will not or cannot work miracles when faith is lacking. For example, Mark records that Jesus could not work many miracles in his home town because people did not believe in him (Mark 6:1–6). By contrast, ancient magicians did not require any trust on the part of their clients. Jesus did not like to be known only as a miracle worker and refused to work wonders on demand; ancient magicians were professionals who publicized their skills. Jesus worked his miracles by a simple command and never tried to manipulate God. Ancient magicians used elaborate spells to compel a spirit to do their will. Jesus never accepted money in exchange for a miracle and only worked miracles to help people. Ancient magicians demanded payment and often called down curses. Jesus' miracles were signs of a larger spiritual reality, the coming of God's kingdom; the alleged wonders of ancient magicians had no theological message.

Jesus apparently taught that the permanence of his exorcisms or cures might depend on spiritual growth in the one healed. According to Matthew's Gospel, Jesus once said that a person who had been exorcised was like an empty house, and if the person did not fill it up, the demon would return, taking along its friends (Matt. 12:43–45). According to John's Gospel, after Jesus healed a paralyzed man, Jesus warned him not to sin again or else something even worse would befall him (John 5:14).

We may now attempt to discern how Jesus worked his miracles by critically examining possible explanations of them. Of course, the most skeptical approach to the miracles of Jesus is to assume that the miracles are completely legendary. On this assumption, Jesus himself did not work any miracles. Instead, the miracle stories arose later thanks to the Church's enthusiastic faith in him. This skeptical view is perhaps particularly associated with David Strauss (1808–1874). It presupposes that miracles are scientifically impossible and that Jesus could not have faked them. Hence, the only remaining alternative is to assume that the miracle stories arose as legends among the faithful after his death. Of course, legends tend to arise around great historical figures, especially among their admirers.

This skeptical view seems untenable today, at least as an explanation for all the miracles. We now realize that science has nothing to tell us about miracles. By definition, a miracle is a unique event caused by a special spiritual intervention. Science only studies repeatable events and ideally studies them under controlled conditions. Of course, by definition a miracle does not take place under controlled conditions. Strauss believed that the gospels originated in the second century, and this late dating allowed time for massive legend to arise. Today scholars generally hold that the gospels were written in the first—not the second—century. Hence, the conclusion seems unavoidable that at the very least, Jesus and his contemporaries already believed that he was working miracles.

Nevertheless, the legendary view can explain some things in the miracle stories. It is apparent that we occasionally find legendary accretions. One obvious example is the stampede of pigs that accompanies the exorcism in Mark 5:1–20. When Jesus is about to expel a "legion" of demons, they ask permission to enter a herd of swine, and Jesus grants it. The herd goes berserk and throws itself off a cliff into a lake and drowns. Such details sound legendary. At least a few miracles in the gospels certainly are not historical at all. The cursing of the fig tree (Mark 11:12–14, 20) will serve as an illustration. It is not credible that Jesus blasted a fig tree for failing to bear fruit when it was not even the right season. Instead, it seems far more likely that Mark adjusted a few details of something Jesus once said about the destruction of an unfruitful fig tree (Luke 13:6–9). With these new details the original parable became a miracle story. In Mark's Gospel that revised story serves to symbolize the temple at Jerusalem. Like the leafy but fruitless tree, the temple looks beautiful but has no substance and is doomed to destruction. It is noteworthy that Mark places Jesus' protest at the temple in the middle of the story of the tree's destruction.

A somewhat less skeptical view about the miracle stories is that Jesus' healings and exorcisms were psychosomatic cures. Of course, at the time people knew little about psychology and assumed that Jesus performed his cures by the power of God. With our modern knowledge, however, we can see that he actually used the power of suggestion. Then after Jesus' death, the historical healings of Jesus helped give rise to legends that he worked even greater wonders. The view that Jesus' historical miracles were psychosomatic cures would be normal among skeptical scholars today.

As a Christian, I have no problem with the claim that psychological suggestion provides at least a partial explanation of how Jesus performed his miracles. Certainly, suggestion can sometimes have a powerful, though perhaps temporary, impact on someone's health. Certainly too, Jesus' healing ministry produced enormous expectations. People believed in him and thought that he could heal them. Therefore, it seems undeniable that psychological suggestion would have been powerfully present.

A crucial ethical issue in all psychosomatic cures is whether the suggestion that leads to healing is in fact true. If a physician gives a patient a sugar pill while claiming that the pill is a newly developed drug, the patient may feel better, but the doctor has lied. Moreover, we may suspect that the sugar pill will bring only transitory relief. By contrast, a true suggestion might bring permanent relief, especially if the sufferer took it permanently to heart.

We may note that Jesus' "suggestions" were true, and medically there is every reason to suppose they would have had a profound impact on the sort of people who often came to him. Jesus "suggested" that God forgave sinners, that God loved the sick, that through Jesus himself, a new spiritual power was available to restore someone to wholeness. Jesus "suggested" that God was inviting sick people to become part of his new community of love and service. As a Christian, I hold that all of these "suggestions" were profoundly true. The gospels make it clear than many of the people that Jesus cured had illnesses that were due to, or complicated by, a deep sense of sinfulness and social isolation. He was especially famous for casting out demons and curing diseases (e.g., menstrual bleeding and "leprosy" [unsightly skin conditions]) that made people ostracized as "socially unclean" and unacceptable to God. Presumably, many of the people who had "demons" suffered from what today we would call debilitating mental problems. Hence, psychologically there is every reason to suppose that Jesus' healing words would in many cases have effected a cure. Moreover, Jesus himself insisted that openness to his larger message (i.e., "faith") was a precondition to receive a miracle from him, and that a healing would only be permanent if people continued to grow spiritually (see earlier discussion on page 67). Consequently, as a Christian I can cheerfully affirm that "suggestion" was at least an important component in some of Jesus' exorcisms and cures. I would add that in our healing efforts today we would do well to give sick people the same "suggestions" that Jesus did.

A still less skeptical view about the miracles is that Jesus—like holy men and women of various traditions—healed by virtue of the special power that comes from extraordinary spiritual growth. It presupposes that "saints" in various traditions (e.g., Tibetan lamas) develop special ("miraculous") powers. Jesus was such a saint and, as a result, could do extraordinary things, though not necessarily more than spiritual masters in non-Christian traditions.

Personally, I have no trouble with the claim that "saints" in various traditions do develop extraordinary powers either from unlocking normally untapped human potential or by becoming channels for spiritual forces from outside. This claim is made by many spiritual traditions, including such "high" religions as Hinduism and Buddhism. It coheres with my own limited experience. As a result of growing spiritually, I have been increasingly able through prayer to channel love and healing power to others, especially through the laying on of hands. Sometimes people feel dramatically better. If even I can do this much, a saint would be able to accomplish far more, especially if the saint had a natural gift for healing. Most people realize only a small percentage of their potential in any area, and certainly some people have a gift for healing. Unfortunately, our own culture tends to be overly skeptical of healing gifts and does not encourage people to pursue the prayer and meditation that would allow those gifts to grow.

Consequently, there is every reason to assume that Jesus' spiritual depth as a "saint" explains at least part of his miraculous powers. Certainly he was a holy man who was in contact with his own full human potential and was also intimate with God and could "channel" divine power. This human potential and divine power must have been at work when he performed miracles. I would especially suggest that Jesus' extraordinary compassion helped heal. It is worth noting that Jesus recognized that other people also had healing power, and he did not question that even some of his critics could cast out "demons" (Luke 11:19).

The question remains whether such saintly powers were all that was at work, and historically and theologically such does not seem to be likely. Jesus claimed that his miracles were greater than those of other people and were signs that through him the kingdom of God was arriving. Of course, as we shall see, the resurrection of Jesus would provide the supreme sign of Jesus' unique status, and the resurrection could not have occurred through Jesus' power as a "saint." Surely, dead saints—no matter how great their spiritual powers—do not raise themselves!

A more traditional Christian belief is that God sometimes gave Jesus the power to work extraordinary miracles that exceeded even what "saints" can do, and these miracles attested Jesus' special mission and relationship to the Father. I believe such to be the case. It is what Jesus and his followers claimed. It does explain extraordinary miracles, especially the feeding of the multitude and the occasional raising of the dead, for which we have considerable historical evidence.[3] It coheres with Jesus' own resurrection, which is the Father's final attestation of him. It also coheres with the church's continuing experience of Jesus' lordship over the universe. It explains the continuing historical fact that some Christians have been able to bear witness to Jesus by working miracles in his name (and not in their own!).

One possible orthodox view is that Jesus worked miracles directly as God, but here I am cautious. Like many modern theologians, I believe that part of the incarnation must have been giving up divine powers. Someone who could work miracles directly as God would not be fully human. Moreover, if Jesus worked miracles directly as God, the historical evidence that he sometimes had difficulty performing them becomes problematic (unless we are prepared to limit God himself). During his human life Jesus apparently did not claim to be God. Hence, I would prefer saying that the miracles of Jesus are the Father's attestation of Jesus' divinity.

NOTES

1. John P. Meier, *A Marginal Jew: Rethinking the Historical Jesus* (3 vols.; New York: Doubleday, 1994), II:874–967.

2. Meier, *A Marginal Jew*, II:537–552.

3. The feeding of the multitude is the only miracle that occurs in each of the gospels, and Matthew and Mark both have two versions of it (Matt. 14:13–21, 15:32–39; Mark 6:30–44, 8:1–9; Luke 9:10–17; John 6:1–14). For a full discussion of the historicity of the feeding miracle see Meier, *A Marginal Jew*, II:950–966, 970. The gospels give us three different stories of Jesus raising the dead, namely Jesus raising the daughter of Jairus (Mark 5:21–24, 35–43), Jesus raising the son of the widow at Nain (Luke 7:11–17),

and Jesus raising Lazarus (John 11:38–44). Each of these stories preserves either the name of someone involved (other than Jesus) or the location where the event occurred. Jesus also refers to himself raising the dead in an independent saying (Matt. 11:4–5). For a full discussion see Meier, II:773–837, 970.

14

The Eucharist in the Life of Jesus and Subsequently

In Jewish Palestine when Jesus was alive, there were at least three besetting problems. First, much of the population lived in dire poverty. The populace had to pay various fees to support the native Jewish hierarchy and had to render taxes to the Romans. These exactions helped reduce many people to bare subsistence. A second enormous social problem was the religious division between the various Jewish sects, including the Pharisees, Sadducees, and Essenes, and the distance between these sects and the majority of the population. The sects differed among themselves over how to interpret religious law and often refused to associate with each other. They also condemned the common people who did not have the resources necessary to pursue the rigorous piety that these sects demanded. Finally, as N. T. Wright has emphasized, there was a gnawing sense that God had not yet returned to dwell among his people and that this divine desertion was manifesting itself in foreign rule and widespread demonic possession.[1]

All of these problems somehow involved food. Much of the population was hungry or even suffering from malnutrition. Religious division especially manifested itself in exclusiveness at meals. The various sects had "pure" meals, which their members shared and which were closed to outsiders. The primary symbol of the hope that God would one day return to Israel was the vision of a final banquet that God would eat with his people.

Jesus preached that with the coming of God's kingdom, these problems would disappear. The hungry would have more than enough to eat (Luke 6:21). Those who had been excluded from Israel would be re-included, and ultimately even the Gentiles would share in salvation (Matt. 8:11). Oppressive hierarchies would disappear. The first would be last, and the last, first. All would know God as their "Father."

Jesus modeled this hoped-for future in his movement. Jesus and his closest followers seem to have had a common purse (John 13:29) that provided for everyone's needs. Jesus insisted on associating with those who had been excluded from pious society (prostitutes, tax collectors, "lepers," and the "demon" possessed). He called God his "Father" and taught that through him, his followers could also address God as "Father."

Jesus symbolized all of his hopes for the future by talking about some final meal. The image of a banquet keeps coming up in the stories (parables) that he told to explain what the coming of God's kingdom would be like. He compared the kingdom to a great supper that a prominent man gave for beggars (Luke 14:15–24), to a barbecue that a grateful father gave when his wayward son returned home (Luke 15:11–32), to a marriage feast for which some people were not prepared (Matt. 25:1–12).

Jesus embodied the longed for future in meals at which he was either the host or the honored guest and at which everyone was welcome. The gospels tell us that a tax collector gave a dinner in Jesus' honor and that his critics took offense at the disreputable guests who attended (Mark 2:13–17). We read that a religious leader invited Jesus to dinner and was scandalized when an immoral woman also arrived (Luke 7:36–50). Jesus himself miraculously and indiscriminately fed thousands of people who came to hear him (e.g., Mark 6:30–44).

Shortly after his demonstration in the temple, Jesus knew that he would soon suffer death, since the nation had rejected his message. He had apparently come to Jerusalem with the hope that he might inspire the nation to prepare for the coming of God's kingdom. The populace had not supported him. He staged a demonstration in the temple that offended the high priests and their followers, and Jerusalem as a whole turned against him. By then he knew that his arrest and execution were inevitable.

To prepare his disciples to continue his mission after his death, Jesus arranged a final meal. There is no good reason to question that the dinner actually occurred. Each of the gospels describes it in some detail (Matt. 26:20–30, Mark 14:17–26, Luke 22:14–38; cf. John 13). Paul, writing only around twenty years later, already regards Jesus' "celebration" of the last supper as a bedrock of Christian tradition (1 Corinthians 10–11, esp., 11:23–25), and Paul personally knew people who apparently had been at that fateful meal.

From the various accounts of the last supper, it seems virtually certain that Jesus said at least three things: He solemnly announced that he would not dine with the disciples again until the next life. He warned them not to betray him and his "covenant" in the meantime. He proclaimed that, henceforth, bread and wine would serve as his body and blood.

Jesus apparently intended to institute a ceremony that would do several things. It would remind the disciples of his message of inclusion and hope. It would give them an opportunity to recommit themselves to living and preaching that message. It would strengthen their expectation of one day being fully reunited with their leader in a renewed world. In the meantime the meal would make their departed leader paradoxically present, especially through bread and wine.

Subsequently, the reenactment of this meal became the central worship service in the church and came to have many names. Roman Catholics call it the "Mass"; the Eastern Orthodox refer to it as the "Divine Liturgy"; Protestants label it the "Lord's Supper" or "Holy Communion." One term that many of the groups use in common is "Eucharist," a word that in Greek means "thanksgiving."

The earliest surviving comments on the Eucharist come from chapters 10–11 of Paul's first letter to the Corinthians and respond to two abuses. The first abuse was the rich's lack of consideration for the poor. Apparently at this early period the Eucharist was the climax of a dinner that Christians ate together. After a common meal, people solemnly received the sacred bread and wine as Christ's body and blood. Unfortunately, people were arriving at different times, and each person or family brought and ate its own food. Not surprisingly, the wealthier members of the congregation could come earlier and ate lavishly. The poor arrived late and had nothing. Paul blasts the Corinthians for putting the poor to shame.

The second abuse was that some Corinthians attended the Eucharist and yet on other occasions participated in Pagan rituals. In response, Paul insists that one cannot eat at the table of the Lord and worship idols. He even goes so far as to suggest that recent illnesses in the congregation are God's punishment for these twin abuses and that the "Eucharist" that the Corinthians are observing can no longer be considered the Lord's Supper.

Paul's comments presuppose that the Eucharist is basically a renewal of a Christian covenant with God. Paul quotes Jesus as saying that the Eucharistic cup is a "new covenant" in his blood (1 Cor. 11:25), and we may note that the Sinai covenant was formalized through blood sacrifices and a meal. Just as the Sinai covenant insisted on the just treatment of the marginal, Paul insists that the Corinthians must not put the poor to shame. Just as the Sinai covenant insisted that the Israelites could only worship one God, Paul insists that the Corinthians cannot share in the "table of the Lord and the table of demons [i.e., idols]" (1 Cor. 10:21). The Sinai covenant established a special bond between the Israelites and God and between one Israelite and another. Paul insists that in the Eucharist we eat Christ's body and drink his blood and thereby become one with him and each other. He writes, "The cup of blessing which we bless, is it not fellowship in the blood of Christ? The bread which we break, is it not fellowship in the body of Christ? Because there is one loaf, we, who are many, are one body" (1 Cor. 10:16–17a).

John's Gospel stresses in chapter 6 that the Eucharist is the continuing sign of the incarnation. The gospel insists that the eternal Word truly became "flesh" (John 1:14). In its comments on the Eucharist the gospel emphasizes this point by making the meal sound like cannibalism. We "munch" on Christ's flesh and drink his blood (John 6:54–56). The theological implications of this extreme rhetoric are evident. In the Eucharist we receive physical food that makes Christ present, and this sacrament is a continuing sign that God became physically present in history through taking on a complete human existence.

In subsequent centuries several doctrines arose to explain how the bread and wine become the body and blood of Jesus in the Eucharistic liturgy. Consubstantiation held that the bread and wine take on the additional property (reality) of being Christ's body and blood. Just as iron when heated gains an additional property without ceasing to be iron, so in the Eucharist the elements remain bread and wine but also become Jesus' flesh and blood. Transubstantiation held that the elements cease to be bread and wine. They only have the appearance of bread and wine but now in reality are Jesus' body and blood. Transignification held that the Eucharistic bread and wine signify the body and blood of Jesus, just as a word stands for something else. Memorialism held that the bread and wine are only the signs through which we recall Christ. More recently, transfinalization has held that the purpose of the Eucharistic bread and wine is the same as the purpose of Christ's body, namely to make God visibly present. Just as a stone becomes a primitive hammer if we use it to drive in a tent peg, so in the context of the liturgy, bread and wine become Christ's body and blood.

Different denominations adopted different Eucharistic doctrines and, partly as a result, stopped allowing other Christians to participate in their liturgies. Catholics opted for transubstantiation; Lutherans, for consubstantiation; and many other Protestants chose memorialism. The different sides tended to misunderstand one another. To Protestants the claim that something ceases to be bread and wine and becomes body and blood sounded like magic. To Catholics the claim that the Eucharist only reminds us of Christ sounded like Christ's body and blood were not present in the liturgy. Consequently, various Christian groups did not allow each other to receive the sacrament. Unfortunately, this exclusiveness persists until the present.

Like some contemporary theologians, I would insist on several points. First, it is enough for Christians to agree that Christ is "really present" in the Eucharist. We do not have to agree on how this happens. Next, we should place renewed emphasis on the covenantal understanding of the Eucharist. That understanding predates the others, is found in scripture, and presumably is what Jesus had in mind. Third, the philosophical categories underlying some of the older theories are inadequate. For example, philosophically, it is dubious to claim that something can fully appear to be one thing and yet in reality be another. An animal that looks just like an eagle cannot be a giraffe.

A more adequate category for sacramental theology would be "symbol." Any ceremony, whether honoring a flag, blessing a marriage, or celebrating a Eucharist, is symbolic. We do something that stands for a larger reality and commitment. Thus, a national flag represents a country and honoring it affirms our respect for that nation. So too when we celebrate the Eucharist, the bread and wine represent Christ, and when we eat the elements, we make our own body his body; that is the place where he dwells and rules. Here we may remember what we saw in the section on baptism: Rituals affect what they symbolize.

If we use the category of symbol we can see that all of the doctrines about how the bread and wine "become" Christ's body and blood are true and compatible. A symbol consists of a signifier (e.g., the word *dog*) and a signified (a hairy, four-legged creature). Hence, consubstantiation is right to insist that the elements of the Eucharist are both bread and wine and the body and blood of Christ. Something can be a symbol only if it stands for something else, and this something else is what is important. By themselves the letters "d," "o," and "g" are only an ink stain. They become a word by standing for an animal. Hence, transubstantiation is correct to insist that the elements of the Eucharist only appear to be bread and wine but in reality are Christ's body and blood.

Transignification, transfinalization, and memorialism are all correct, because as a symbol the Eucharist signifies (stands for) the body and blood of Christ, has the same "purpose" as Christ's body (i.e., to make God visibly present), and helps us recall who Christ was and what he did for us.

When we celebrate a Eucharist, we basically remember, recommit, look forward, and presently embody. We remember all that God has done for us, beginning with the creation of the world. We especially focus on the incarnation, the last supper, the crucifixion, the resurrection, and the gift of the Spirit. We recommit ourselves to faithfulness to Jesus and his vision of the kingdom. This faithfulness includes loving God and one another, working for justice and mercy, and being part of a community to which ideally all Christians should belong. We look forward to the coming of final salvation, namely, our individual resurrection at death and the ultimate triumph of justice, peace, and faith in Jesus on earth. As we do all these things, we worship in the Spirit of the risen Christ, and in doing so embody him.

The Eucharist, as the central act of Christian worship, normally includes many types of prayer, but each of them takes on an additional dimension. In the Eucharistic liturgy we confess our sins. We pray for others, especially those in great need. We listen prayerfully to readings from the Bible. We give thanks for God's blessings. Nevertheless, all of these prayers have a special quality, since they are part of our celebration of what Christ did for us and our recommitment to be his body in this world.

NOTES

1. N. T. Wright, *Jesus and the Victory of God* (Minneapolis, MN: Fortress, 1996), 615–624.

15

The Death of Jesus and the Doctrine of the Atonement

It is historically certain that Jesus was crucified. The crucifixion is the most attested fact about him. It is prominent not only in the gospels but throughout the New Testament. It also appears in brief notes about him by both the Jewish historian Josephus and the Pagan historian Tacitus. Moreover, the church would never have invented a story about its founder suffering public rejection and shameful death.

Unfortunately, it is uncertain why the authorities chose to execute Jesus. Specifically, at least three viewpoints are historically plausible. One possible view is that the Romans were responsible for the death of Jesus. They executed him because they regarded him as a possible royal pretender. Jesus had proclaimed the coming of God's kingdom and at least implicitly acted as its head. Would-be messiahs had already been a problem for the Romans in occupied Palestine, and government policy was to kill them. Whether or not Jesus was actually a threat to their rule, the Roman authorities saw him as a risk. Then at his trial Jesus confirmed their fears by admitting that in some sense he did claim to be a "king." Consequently, the Romans concluded that they should execute him. The gospels try to shift blame onto the Jews in an attempt to avoid persecution by making Christianity look less dangerous to the government.

A second possible view is that the Jewish high priests were responsible for the death of Jesus. All the gospels insist that it was the high priests who arrested and condemned Jesus and pressured the Roman governor to order his execution. The high priests would certainly have regarded some of the claims of Jesus as blasphemous. For example, Jesus had insisted that people could receive God's forgiveness simply by coming to him.[1] Conventional Judaism taught that sinners must offer a sacrifice in the temple to be reconciled to God, and such sacrifices helped enrich the high priests. The formal charge against Jesus at the hearing before the high priest seems to have been blasphemy (e.g., Mark 14:63–64). The high priests also had compelling political reasons to destroy Jesus. The power of the high priests depended on the Jewish populace revering them as God's representatives and on the Romans tolerating them as leaders who would prevent revolt. Jesus had implicitly undercut people's reverence for the priests. He had attacked religious privilege and hypocrisy. He predicted the destruction of the temple and symbolized his prophecy by staging a violent protest in the temple courts—and the temple was the foundation for both priestly authority and revenue. The high priests feared a potential revolutionary even more than the Romans did, because they knew that a revolt would force the Romans to eliminate native rule altogether, thus ending priestly authority. John's Gospel explicitly records that the priests feared that Jesus' miracles would lead the populace to acclaim him and rebel and that the ultimate result would be Roman repression, including the destruction of the temple. This fear made the Jewish leadership decide that Jesus must die (John 11:47–53).

A third possible explanation for the crucifixion of Jesus is that the Jewish populace in Jerusalem turned against him when he attacked violent national aspirations. This explanation especially comes from N. T. Wright, and I will augment his argument.[2] Jesus lived in a time of great polarization. The Jewish people as a whole resented Roman rule whether directly through Roman governors in the south or indirectly through the Herods in the north. "Respectable" Jews attempted to preserve their national heritage by demanding that everyone keep the biblical laws that made Jews visibly different from Gentiles and by teaching their children to regard outsiders as unclean. Jesus undercut both efforts since he was casual about legal observance and freely associated with the "unclean," including tax collectors for the hated government. Underlying Jesus' behavior was the conviction that Jews could only overcome oppression by loving their oppressors. Jesus spent most of his ministry in the north, and, as a result, the populace of Jerusalem was unsure of his intentions. Many people hoped that he would support a revolt, and they acclaimed him when he arrived. However, Jesus dashed their hopes in his protest at the temple. For the populace of Jerusalem, the temple was the very symbol of national aspirations, since it celebrated Israel's God and emphasized the importance of Jewish purity. Jesus' demonstration attacked this understanding of the temple. Mark records that Jesus insisted that the temple was to be a place of prayer for all nations (Mark 11:17). His protest symbolized that using the temple as a stronghold for nationalism would ultimately lead to the building's destruction. Indeed, he declared that the temple had become a lair for "bandits," and "bandit" was a pejorative label for a violent revolutionary. The populace responded with outrage and demanded his crucifixion, which the Roman governor reluctantly granted when a riot threatened.

In my opinion there is a measure of truth in each of these positions. Certainly, the Roman authorities were partly responsible for the crucifixion. The formal charge against Jesus was treason against Rome, attempting to become "King of the Jews." The Roman governor heard the case, found Jesus guilty, and ordered his execution. The effort of the evangelists to exculpate the Romans is unconvincing. For example, in Matthew's Gospel, Pontius Pilate even washes his hands and declares publicly that he is innocent of Jesus' blood (Matt. 27:24). Such a scene cannot be historical. Whatever Pilate's personal views about Jesus may have been, he could not as the Roman governor have publicly proclaimed that he was engaging in a miscarriage of justice! The high priests were also partly responsible. As we have seen, they had every reason to get rid of Jesus, especially after his attack on the temple. The high priests were the ones who arrested him and presented him to Pilate. Nevertheless, the populace in Jerusalem must share the blame. The high priests could not have taken action against Jesus without popular acquiescence. The gospels make it clear that the authorities feared an uprising during the Passover celebration and initially hesitated to move against Jesus. They changed their minds after he lost support.

Only the hostility of a nationalistic crowd can explain the otherwise puzzling fact that in connection with the trial of Jesus the Roman governor freed Barabbas, a convicted rebel. Neither the governor nor the high priests could have desired such a release. The only plausible explanation is that Pilate had to placate a nationalistic crowd who was angrily demanding Jesus' crucifixion.

Unfortunately, in subsequent history the church used Jewish involvement in the death of Jesus as an excuse for antisemitism with catastrophic results. Of course, Christianity began as a Jewish denomination, since Jesus and all his first followers were Jews. But it was perhaps inevitable that it would become a separate religion after the crucifixion. Naturally, the Jewish authorities could not support a movement whose founder they had helped execute. Once the communities separated, further tension arose since each group claimed exclusive right to the Hebrew Scriptures. The Jewish community insisted that the scriptures supported its claim to be God's continuing chosen people. The church insisted that those same scriptures predicted the coming of Jesus as the Messiah who would convert the world. Nevertheless, the church heightened the schism by emphasizing Jewish guilt for the crucifixion. Initially, this emphasis was in part politically motivated. The church wanted to minimize Roman responsibility so that Christianity would appear harmless to the imperial government. The tragic result was that Christians often saw Jews as Christ-killers. This perception helped motivate centuries of persecution that culminated with the Holocaust. Nazism inherited antisemitism from the church, even if Nazism was not itself a Christian movement.

From a theological perspective, blaming the Jews for the crucifixion of Jesus was singularly inappropriate. As we shall see in a moment, the church insisted that the death of Jesus brought *salvation* to the world because he died for the sins of *all* people. Consequently, to blame the Jews for the death of Jesus implicitly undercut the church's message that the crucifixion was part of God's merciful plan to deliver humanity from the consequences of everyone's faults.

Today it seems best to view Jewish involvement in the crucifixion as a warning to the church itself not to engage in the persecution of religious dissenters. Judaism was Jesus' own sacred community. He challenged it with the hope that it would repent.

Hence, to Christians the crucifixion should be a constant reminder of the dangers of eliminating people who question our own theological orthodoxy and social complacency.

Traditionally, Christians have held that through the incarnation and crucifixion, God overcame sin and its consequences for humanity. Because of human sin, we were estranged from God, and salvation was impossible. Jesus' birth, suffering, and death reconciled God and humanity and produced atonement (literally, "at-one-ment," making us and God one again) for the world. Such atonement not only changed our present lives but made it possible for us to receive God's forgiveness at the last judgment and have everlasting beatitude.

Over the centuries there have been various theories as to how Jesus made atonement, and the church has never taken an official position over which (if any) is correct. The physical theory held that Jesus restored the divine image in humanity. According to this perspective, God made the first people in his own image. However, due to their sin, Adam and Eve lost the divine image, and all their descendants lacked it. As the incarnation of God, Jesus had the divine image, and Christians receive it by being incorporated into him through baptism. The ransom, satisfaction, and penal substitution theories all basically held that Jesus bore the penalty for our sin. According to these theories, sin must be punished. By our sin we have either given Satan the legal right to possess us, which must somehow be respected; offended God's honor, which must be restored; or violated divine justice, which must be upheld. Jesus delivers us from our deserved punishment by taking the punishment on himself. He either ransoms us from Satan or restores God's offended honor or pays the legal penalty for our sin. In any case, we receive the benefits of Jesus' freely chosen and totally undeserved suffering.

Today it is difficult to accept any of the theories listed above if we take them literally. The physical theory does not explain exactly what the divine image consisted of and how it could have been lost through sin. Moreover, the Bible explicitly states that even after Adam and Eve's fall, humans still had the divine image (e.g., Gen. 5:3). The ransom, satisfaction, and penal substitution theories fail to explain why "justice" is necessary and how Jesus' suffering and death restore it. Thus, as Abelard already argued in the Middle

Ages, Satan has no legal rights over us, no matter how much we sinned, since he tempted us and is, therefore, more guilty than we are. The suffering and death of the wholly innocent Jesus cannot be pleasing to God and, therefore, cannot restore his honor. There is no need for "justice" once human beings recognize their sin and repent. God can simply be merciful.

Nevertheless, the theories of the atonement discussed remain helpful if we see them from a psychological and social perspective. Thus, the physical theory is correct once we substitute role model for some vague "divine image," and realize that the crucified Jesus provides us with the supreme model of a human being filled with God. Unfortunately, due to sin, societies hold up other models for people to imitate. American entertainment, for example, provides violent men as role models for boys and sexy movie stars as models for girls. Such models even infect morality and religion. Thus, fighting for one's country, rather than working for peace, becomes the moral ideal, and God becomes a justification for war, even wars of aggression. The belt buckles of Nazi soldiers read "God with us." By contrast, the incarnation holds up self-sacrificing compassion as the model for how a human being ideally should behave and as the model for how God always acts. Thus, Jesus incarnates the "divine image" in humans and challenges us to adopt that image in our personal and communal lives.

Similarly, the ransom, satisfaction, and penal theories of the atonement are correct once we realize that Jesus' death placates our need for "justice" rather than God or Satan's. Psychologically and socially, we are tempted to believe that we must always punish wrongdoing. We focus on retribution rather than bringing sinners to repentance and reform. Consequently, "justice" degenerates into public vengeance. We then project our values on God and insist that God demands the death penalty. We even exact retribution from ourselves. We punish ourselves for our failures, and think that we should feel guilty and that such feelings please God. The death of Jesus undermines all such temptations. It shows that God accepted the ultimate humiliation without demanding vengeance, and it invites us to give up retribution as a moral goal. In Luke's Gospel we read that Jesus forgave his executioners (Luke 23:34), and in the Acts we see Stephen imitating Jesus' example as he is being unjustly killed (Acts 7:60). Moreover, God's love for sinners as shown on the cross demands that we love others and ourselves for his sake. As Christians we do not love others and ourselves because people are inherently beautiful or because there are always extenuating circumstances that justify people's wrongdoing. We love others and ourselves because God loves everyone, and through God's power we believe that everyone has at least the potential to become beautiful.

The classical theory of the atonement that remains especially helpful today is the moral exemplary theory. The medieval theologian Peter Abelard (1079–1142) first formulated it, and it continues to be popular. Indeed, I have repeatedly drawn on it in earlier discussion in attempting to place other atonement theories in a more modern perspective.

The theory holds that the crucifixion overcomes sin simply by demonstrating how great God's love for us is and, as a consequence, inspiring us to love. The incarnation and especially the cross show that God will always love us, no matter how much we sin against him. This love leads us to love him and, in imitation of Christ, to love others, even our enemies. Such love produces genuine goodness. Instead of doing what is right merely to escape public censure, personal guilt feelings, or eternal damnation, we love from the heart. This freer love bonds us more closely to God and thereby makes us signs of God's supreme love for others.

I would add that the cross also demonstrates that there is real injustice, and we must not blame victims. We are continually tempted to insist that everything that happens is somehow just. This insistence allows us to claim that our political and social systems are functioning well, and the universe is basically fair. These comforting assertions help keep us from looking at our personal and collective sin and give us an excuse for not aiding people who are in misery. Even some of the high religions make the mistake of assuming that only the evil suffer. Thus, in response to apparent innocent suffering, Hinduism and Buddhism claim that good people who suffer are now paying the price for misdeeds in previous incarnations. For Christians, the cross makes such comforting assumptions impossible. Jesus was the supremely righteous person and the incarnation of a totally loving God. Yet he suffered torture and death. Hence, he provides the ultimate proof that the world—and especially the structures of power—can be horrendously wicked, and that many sufferers are innocent. This proof must in turn spur us to greater efforts to help those whom the "system" has unjustly crushed.

Finally, I would also argue that by becoming a human being and experiencing suffering and death, God gave us a deeper basis for bonding to him by sharing in a common struggle. All human beings are vulnerable and mortal, and most of us must endure debilitating suffering at some point. Only by becoming human could God experience firsthand what we must experience. Hence, the incarnation gives God a deeper bond with us. Community is not some vague feeling of euphoria; it is what we have been through together. Those who must suffer—and basically that is everyone—can find comfort in the awareness that God through the incarnation also suffered and truly understands what it means to be crushed. It is also a great consolation to people who must suffer in response to God's call that God does not ask more of them than he asked of himself and that when they suffer for doing what is right they are growing ever more like him.

We must now return briefly to the issue of how we can believe in God when there is so much undeserved suffering in the world. Many people feel that here we have the fatal objection to ethical monotheism. A powerful and good God would never allow all the undeserved misery that we see in the world—and, perhaps especially, have seen in the horrors of the modern era.

We may note in passing that denying the existence of God makes the problem of undeserved suffering worse, not better. Atheism does not provide an answer to the philosophical question of why there is innocent suffering but instead claims that there is no answer. Hence, the very urgency with which we ask the question is itself an objection to atheism. Atheism makes it more difficult to bear undeserved misery. Even if a theist does not know why the innocent suffer, at least a theist has faith that suffering has some legitimate explanation and purpose, and this faith gives comfort. By contrast, the claim that innocent suffering lacks any ultimate meaning inspires cynicism.

The incarnation and crucifixion suggest that God "allows" innocent suffering for two reasons. One explanation is that God voluntarily limited himself in the process of creating the world. The incarnation and crucifixion demonstrate that God freely took on the limitations of becoming human and submitting to debilitating misery. Perhaps, therefore, when God created the world and gave it autonomy, he also freely limited his ability to change things in it. Hence, God often lacks the power to eliminate innocent suffering. Of course, an objection to this explanation is that God sometimes can and, in my opinion, does work miracles.

A second explanation for why God "allows" innocent suffering is that God primarily wants the world to discover his existence through self-sacrificing love rather than through constant divine interventions. Miracles are only signs, and they must be rare if they are to remain that way. The definitive proof of the existence of God is the love shown by Jesus on the cross and the love that Christians show in response. This explanation suggests that the supreme task of human history is for human beings to search for God and find him through love. I believe this to be the case. As a teacher myself, I think of human history as analogous to a classroom discussion in which the primary topic is God. In a typical school discussion, the teacher challenges the students to solve a problem even though the teacher already knows the answer. By figuring out the answer for themselves, the students learn how to think and especially learn the proper methodology for dealing with the matter under consideration. In the discussion ideally each student makes a contribution, and the collective quest unites the class. If the class is totally lost, the teacher may give a few hints to get the discussion back on track. However, the teacher cannot plainly tell the students the answer without ending the discussion and depriving the students of the privilege of discovering something for themselves. So too I believe that all of human history is a giant discussion in which we are collectively struggling to find the answers to many questions. The discussion goes on from generation to generation. The common quest unites us, and ideally every person makes a unique contribution. Of course, some of the questions that we struggle with are scientific or artistic and so forth. Nevertheless, as a Christian, I believe that the most important question of all is whether there is a God and, if so, what he is like. Everyone is supposed to make a contribution to discovering the answer. God wishes us to learn collectively for ourselves that the proper methodology to answer the central question of human existence is love. Through love we are to discover the God who is supreme love. Sometimes when history gets too far off track, God gives hints, such as occasional miracles or, especially recently, near-death experiences. Yet God cannot unmistakably reveal himself through constant interventions to end innocent suffering without ending the discussion, and the discussion is too vital to be cut short.

NOTES

1. E. P. Sanders has especially emphasized this point. See E. P. Sanders, *The Historical Figure of Jesus* (London: Allen Lane Penguin, 1993), 235–236.

2. N. T. Wright, *Jesus and the Victory of God* (Minneapolis, MN: Fortress, 1996), 413–424, 549.

16

✣

The Historical Problem of Whether Jesus Rose from the Dead

It is difficult for historians to know how to respond to a well documented claim that something "impossible" happened. On the one hand, a historian might assume that the stupendous event could not have occurred despite the evidence and that, therefore, in this case there was a bizarre blunder. On the other hand, a historian could argue that the stupendous event shows that our assumptions about what is possible or even real are mistaken.

Analogous problems arise in science. When scientists observe something that present theory cannot account for, they must ask whether the observations are erroneous or whether our understanding of the universe needs modification. For example, when astronomers first noticed that the orbit of the planet Mercury was not following accepted scientific law, they thought that the observations might be mistaken. Then Einstein hypothesized that the law itself had serious deficiencies. Fundamental reality differed from what everyone had previously thought. Subsequent experiments proved Einstein correct.

The resurrection of Jesus provides the supreme example of the historical problem of how to account for an "impossible" event. The gospels insist that a woman named Mary Magdalene and some female companions witnessed Jesus' burial. On the following Sunday they went to the site and discovered that the tomb was now empty. Then Jesus himself appeared to various people and proved to them that he was alive. So far as I am aware, there is no other reasonably well attested claim that someone rose from the grave. Consequently, one must either assume that the early Christian statements about Jesus' resurrection were wildly inaccurate or that God actually did raise Jesus from the dead with all the larger implications that this supreme miracle would necessitate.

Let us evaluate the evidence systematically. We will begin with the story of the empty tomb and then go on to the appearances.

Skeptics often argue that the New Testament story of the discovery of the empty tomb is a legend. The resurrection "appearances"—whatever they may have been—had persuaded the disciples that Jesus was alive. It was then only natural for Christians to imagine that someone had gone to his grave and found it empty. The earliest written presentation of the resurrection is in 1 Corinthians 15 and does not explicitly mention the empty tomb. Jesus himself had been a storyteller, and the early Christian movement was creative, as the discrepancies between the different accounts of the resurrection experiences themselves demonstrate. The Romans did not usually return the bodies of executed criminals, and Mary Magdalene and her companions were visitors to Jerusalem. Consequently, the burial site could have been lost, and Christians were free to assume and proclaim that it was now empty.

Nevertheless, it seems to me that the preponderance of the historical evidence makes it *extremely likely* that in fact Jesus' tomb was empty. The silence of 1 Corinthians should not be overestimated. The passage explicitly states that Jesus "was buried" and "raised" (1 Cor. 15:4). These words clearly imply faith in the physical resurrection of Jesus and may even imply knowledge of the empty tomb. There are signs that the story of the tomb's discovery was early and widespread. The gospels of Mark and John have independent versions of it. In both cases the authors were using older material, since they edited it by inserting their own perspectives. It is not likely that the location of the tomb was forgotten, because the gospel accounts of the burial are credible. We may especially note that if the church had not known who buried Jesus, it would not have claimed that he belonged to the circles who engineered Jesus' execution (see Luke 23:50–51). It is most improbable that a late Christian legend would have attributed the finding of the tomb to women. In the first century the testimony of women was considered unreliable. Indeed, women could not be witnesses in a Jewish trial. Of course, we could be dealing with an early apologetic legend that originated at a time when it was still known that only the women remained in Jerusalem. Nevertheless, this hypothesis faces severe difficulties. Such a legend would have begun and circulated when Mary Magdalene and her companions were still alive and knew that it was false. Moreover, there is no evidence that the males fled from *Jerusalem*. All the gospels at least clearly imply that the males were still in the city on Easter, and Matthew and Mark merely suggest that *at some later point* the church returned to Galilee where there was a resurrection appearance.

Historically, it is virtually certain that Jesus' disciples "saw" something that they understood to be Jesus risen from the grave. In 1 Corinthians 15:4–8, Paul lists the people to whom the risen Christ "appeared." Paul explicitly states that most of the witnesses were still alive and thereby implicitly invited his original readers to consult them. Moreover, Paul lists himself as a witness to the resurrection, and we should note that the experience converted him. Previously, he was an enemy of the Christian movement.

Skeptics argue that the resurrection experiences were subjective. The original disciples were traumatized by the crucifixion. They desperately wanted to believe that their teacher was not dead. As a result, they suffered from hallucinations that convinced them that he had risen. As an enemy of the church prior to his conversion, Paul learned about claims that Jesus had appeared to others. As is typical of persecutors, Paul had a conflicted personality. Then he too had a psychological "break" that he interpreted as an appearance of Jesus.

Nevertheless, there are difficulties with the argument that the appearances were hallucinations. In Jewish tradition there was no precedent to enable people to imagine the resurrection of an individual before the end of the world. The normal way to console oneself over the death of a martyr was to look for God to punish those responsible and perhaps to reward the martyr on the last day. An empty tomb does not normally lead to visions of a resurrection. If I went to my parents' grave and found it empty, I would not have such a vision and certainly would not conclude they had physically risen from the dead! The accounts of the resurrection appearances stress that those who witnessed them were startled and initially incredulous. Jesus had taught his disciples the danger of hypocrisy and the need for discernment, and we may question whether his followers would have easily been deceived by a subjective experience. Moreover, none of the accounts of the resurrection appearances tells us that the followers of Jesus were having an "inner" experience. Instead, our sources claim that in many of the resurrection appearances more that one person was present and Jesus was somehow visible to everyone. Elsewhere Matthew is enthusiastic about dreams and elsewhere Luke is enthusiastic about visions, but neither evangelist suggests that the resurrection experiences were in any sense dreams or visions. Finally, if the resurrection experiences resulted from natural causes, we should have other instances of groups proclaiming that their dead founders physically rose from the grave. So far as I am aware, no such examples exist.

By contrast, it is likely that the resurrection accounts that stress the undeniable physical presence of Jesus are not historical in the strict sense. Luke's Gospel tells us that the risen Jesus ate a piece of broiled fish before the disciples to prove that he was not a ghost (Luke 24:36–43). John's Gospel records that Jesus actually challenged a disciple named Thomas to touch the wounds of the crucifixion (John 20:24–29). Such stories only appear in individual gospels, and it is noteworthy that Luke and John wrote after Mark and Paul. If such physical events had actually occurred, their absence in the earlier tradition is hard to explain. On the other hand, one can easily explain their origin through apologetic and theological interests. The church had to reply to Jewish allegations that the disciples stole the corpse (note Matt. 27:62–66, 28:11–15) and radical Christian allegations that Jesus did not have a body (e.g., 2 John 7). I believe that such stories of undeniable proof are valid interpretations of the significance of the resurrection. They dramatically underline the Christian claim that Jesus physically rose from the dead. Such stories may even be translations into earthly terms of experiences that differed fundamentally from normal reality. The risen Christ was so tangibly real that it was as if he could have eaten a piece of fish or as if someone could have touched his wounds. Nevertheless, we probably should not assume that if a photographer had been present we would have a picture of these events.

We may now attempt to give a description of what the resurrection experiences basically were. Building on the work of Charles Austin Perry, we can note that there is a pattern in most of the accounts.[1] First, we have a mysterious presence that initially can be doubted or misunderstood. Then Jesus makes it clear beyond all question that he himself is present. Jesus issues a command to the disciples to share the glorious news that he is risen. With that command there is a promise that, if the witnesses obey, Jesus will somehow support them and confirm their message. Thus, in Matthew 28:16–20 when Jesus first appears, some disciples are doubtful. Then Jesus comes and speaks to them. He orders them to go and convert all nations and promises to be with the disciples until the conclusion of the world. We see the same pattern in Luke 24:36–49. When Jesus appears, the disciples initially fear that they are seeing a ghost. He dispels all doubt by inviting them to examine his hands and feet and by eating a piece of fish. He then tells them that they are to proclaim to all nations that repentance and forgiveness are available in his name. He promises that soon they will receive the Holy Spirit to empower them for this mission. Because all, or at least most, of the four elements—mysterious presence, recognition that Jesus is certainly present, command, and promise—appear in account after account, we may conclude that the actual experiences probably contained them.

Theologically, this pattern suggests that Christians can verify in their own experience that Jesus has risen from the dead by obeying his commands and awaiting the promise. The resurrection appearances were privileged encounters. Only a few people received them. But the command and the promise seem more general. Jesus also commands us to follow him, and he promises that if we do so, he will support us. If we obey the command, we will receive the promise and know that he has risen from the dead and rules the universe.

As the above suggests, the historical evidence for the resurrection remains an indispensable sign—but only a sign. Without the testimony of the original witnesses to the resurrection, we would never have deduced that Jesus rose physically from the grave. However, the testimony only makes the resurrection extremely likely. Additional proof of the resurrection must come through our own individual and communal spiritual experience. Here we have the answer to the skeptical question of why Jesus did not prove his resurrection definitively by, say, appearing to the Roman governor or the Jewish high priest. The testimony of the resurrection is not a substitute for faith; it is an invitation to be open to the possibility of faith. Faith depends on a personal relationship with God that deepens as we trust his call and do his will.

NOTES

1. Charles Austin Perry, *The Resurrection Promise: An Interpretation of the Easter Narratives* (Grand Rapids, MI: Eerdmans, 1986), passim, e.g., 37.

17

✠

The Significance of the Resurrection for the Early Church

Traditionally, Christians have distinguished between the resurrection, the ascension, and coming of the Holy Spirit, and the liturgical calendar devotes a different date to each. The resurrection is commemorated on Easter Sunday and celebrates Jesus' return to life. Because the resurrection occurred on a Sunday, Sunday displaced the Jewish Sabbath as the weekly Christian holy day. The ascension is commemorated on the fortieth day after Easter (or the nearest Sunday) and celebrates Jesus' triumphant entrance into heaven where he received universal authority. The coming of the Holy Spirit is commemorated on the fiftieth day after Easter and celebrates Jesus' mysterious return to the church in the Spirit.

These traditional distinctions are based on the narrative in Luke through Acts. Luke especially underlines the physical return of Jesus himself at Easter. The risen Jesus insists to his disciples that he is not a ghost and invites them to handle him to verify that he is the same person they had known (Luke 24:36–43). In his sequel to the gospel, the Acts of the Apostles, Luke tells us that after Jesus had appeared to his disciples over a forty-day period, he was taken up in their sight into heaven (Acts 1:3–11). Then in the second chapter of Acts, we read that on the Jewish feast of Pentecost, which would have been fifty days after the resurrection, the Spirit of Jesus wonderfully came down on the disciples and filled them. The gift of the Holy Spirit enabled them to proclaim the Christian message to the world. The church took over Luke's time line and used it as the foundation for much of the traditional ecclesiastical calendar.

Originally, however, the resurrection, ascension, and the coming of the Holy Spirit were more like different aspects of a single event, as other New Testament texts make clear. For example, in John's Gospel the resurrection, the ascension, and the coming of the Holy Spirit apparently occur on the same day. Before sunrise Mary Magdalene meets the risen Jesus. He tells her not to hold him up because he must ascend to the Father and that Mary is to tell the disciples that he is ascending (20:11–18). Then on Easter night Jesus appears to the disciples as a group and gives them the Holy Spirit (20:19–23). Similarly in Matthew there is no distinction between the resurrection, ascension, and the coming of the Holy Spirit. In the gospel's final scene when Jesus appears to the apostles, he declares that he has already received universal authority. He immediately sends them out to preach with the assurance that he will remain with them always (Matt. 28:16–20).

As the above suggests, the New Testament accounts of the resurrection encounters are translations of events that could not be described literally. We cannot give a literal description of something that drastically differs from anything that people have experienced. If a congenitally blind person asks us to describe shocking pink, we will not be able to respond helpfully by discussing how it contrasts with other shades of pink, because the blind person has never seen any color. Instead, we will have to translate the experience into some frame of reference that the blind person has experienced. We can say that shocking pink is like the blast of an electric guitar or the taste of a hot pepper. The great discrepancies between the various accounts of the resurrection experiences make it evident that they are translations. The New Testament authors use different metaphors to give us some sense of what the experiences were.

By translating the resurrection into resurrection, ascension, and the coming of the Holy Spirit, Luke through Acts stresses several theological points. The resurrection emphasizes the identity of the risen Lord with the earthly Jesus (Luke 24:39). The Jesus who appears to the disciples is the same Jesus they have always known. He shows them the wounds of the cross and eats a piece of fish. The ascension emphasizes that Jesus has been glorified and reigns in heaven as Lord. In the Acts of the Apostles, Stephen, shortly before his death, has a vision of Jesus standing on the right side of God in paradise (Acts 7:56). Because Jesus is in heaven, he is no longer with us in the same way that historically he was, and we must await his triumphant return. The coming of the Spirit stresses that, nevertheless, Jesus is present with us in a new way, bringing to us power, joy, and vocation.

Luke's schema is not merely a theological construct but is based on the actual resurrection experiences and their early interpretation, as we can see from other New Testament documents. John's Gospel, for instance, clearly assumes that the risen Jesus is the same person that the disciples had known. Indeed, Jesus invites Thomas to examine the wounds of the cross (John 20:27). This physical Jesus has now departed, and, because he has departed, he has given us the Holy Spirit to replace him. In chapter 14 Jesus assures his followers that he is going away to prepare an eternal home for them (14:3) and that he will give the disciples the Spirit who will remain with them forever (14:16–17). Later Jesus even insists that the Holy Spirit cannot come until he himself has left (16:7). Luke's own account of the ascension and Pentecost probably was based on specific historical events. The ascension in Acts may well be an edited version of a specific resurrection appearance, and the account of Pentecost is surely an edited version of an occasion on which a crowd of Christians felt especially empowered by the Spirit shortly after the resurrection appearances.

Consequently, we will use Luke's categories to analyze the resurrection experiences and will note the theological implications that the early church drew from them. We will start with the resurrection. It is clear that "resurrection" (i.e., that it was Jesus himself who had risen) was an integral part of the complex Easter experience. All our texts explicitly state, or at least clearly assume, that the person who appeared to the disciples was none other than the Jesus they had always known. Without that identity the resurrection appearances would not have had their amazement and joy.

From the conviction that Jesus the human being had risen, the church drew two conclusions. First, the rest of us will rise to glory if we imitate the self-sacrifice that Jesus showed by accepting crucifixion. As Paul wrote to the Romans, "If we have died with Christ, we believe that we also will live with him" (Rom. 6:8).

First-century Judaism debated whether there was personal survival after death. The Pharisees affirmed it; the Sadducees denied it. No such debate ever occurred in the early church. The resurrection of Jesus proved that there was resurrection and showed that the way for others to obtain it was by imitating Jesus' self-giving love. The church also concluded, erroneously it turned out, that the general resurrection was near. For a few decades, Christians lived in eager expectation that Christ would return soon to raise the dead physically from their graves. Most Jews had believed that one day there would be a general resurrection. Jesus' own resurrection led Christians to think that it was imminent.

Belief in the "ascension," namely that Jesus has gone to heaven where he now reigns over the universe, had a least two bases in early Christian experience. First, the risen Lord whom people encountered was undeniably divine. New Testament resurrection texts tend to equate the risen Jesus with God despite the theological problems involved. In the final scene in Matthew's Gospel Jesus declares that he has "all authority in heaven and on earth" and that the disciples should baptize people "in the Name [singular!] of the Father and the Son and the Holy Spirit" (Matt. 28:16–20). In John's Gospel when Thomas sees the risen Jesus, Thomas exclaims "My Lord and my God!" (John 20:28). In his letter to the Philippians, Paul insists, "God highly exalted him [Jesus] and granted to him the Name that is above every name, that at the Name of Jesus every knee might bend of things in heaven and on earth and under the earth and every tongue confess that Jesus Christ is Lord" (Phil. 2:9–11). Historically, it is astonishing that monotheistic Jews could have claimed that a flesh-and-blood person whom they had actually known was in fact God. Yet, the resurrection texts do that. The only possible explanation in that part of the resurrection experience is that Jesus was divine. We may especially note that the basic structure of the encounters with the risen Christ resembles the basic structure of the paradigmatic appearance of God to Moses in Exodus 3. When God appears to Moses and reveals the divine name, we have the pattern of (1) a presence that initially can be misunderstood or doubted, (2) the subsequent certainty that this "presence" is God, (3) a command to make God and his will known, and (4) a promise that if the command is obeyed God will support him. Thus, Moses first sees a burning bush and is puzzled.

Then God identifies himself. He commands Moses to go to Egypt and set the Israelites free. Moses hesitates, and God promises to be with him. As we saw above, the same pattern of mysterious presence, certainty, command, and promise also occurs when Jesus appears after his resurrection. Hence, it is not surprising that his followers concluded that he was divine. Moreover, in the resurrection accounts, as during his ministry, Jesus acts with God's authority and yet does not appeal to God to authenticate that authority. In other words, Jesus acts as God himself.

The second basis of the ascension was the experience that after a time the series of special appearances stopped, and it seemed that Jesus had definitively departed. When Paul wrote to the Corinthians in the fifties of the first century, he listed the resurrection appearances. He insisted that his own, which occurred two decades earlier, was the "last" (1 Cor. 15:4–8). Consequently, it was clear that Jesus was alive but no longer physically on earth. The only possible explanation for this paradox was that Jesus now was in heaven.

From the ascension, the church drew several important conclusions. First, the followers of Jesus had a heavenly advocate with the Father. Their leader was at the Father's side interceding for them. Of course, the ascension also showed that God had vindicated Jesus' life and teaching and that they should be a model for us. Finally, the ascension suggested that the death of Jesus must somehow have overcome the evil powers of the universe, since Jesus now reigned with divine authority. This last conclusion would ultimately lead to the doctrine of the atonement, which is discussed earlier.

The conclusion that the risen Christ has sent his Spirit was based on the experience that Jesus' transforming call and energy continued to be available. After the resurrection appearances, the people who witnessed them continued to feel Christ's presence but in a different way. He was no longer tangibly there, but he still summoned his followers to love and service, and his divine energy vibrantly enabled them to respond. That Spirit inspired joy and enthusiasm and an outpouring of gifts, such as inspired preaching and an ever-growing understanding of who Jesus was. Christians had a deep sense of community with one another in the Lord and a sense that now he was conforming them to his divine self. Even people who had not been privileged to have encounters with the risen Lord could receive this transforming power.

From the presence of the Spirit the first Christians drew reassuring conclusions. Christians were already experiencing some of the supreme blessings of the age of fulfillment. In the Old Testament various prophets foretold an outpouring of the Spirit (cf., e.g., Joel 2:28ff; Acts 2:16–21). Now it had taken place. But if the Spirit was already present, there was no need for the world to end at once. The church may have been eager for Jesus to return but also knew that the church itself was already his body on earth, because his Spirit dwelt in the fellowship. The presence of the Spirit confirmed that Jesus' resurrection was real. Jesus could only have given the Spirit if he himself was alive. The presence of the Spirit even verified that Jesus was divine, since his Spirit was God's Spirit. Like God himself the Spirit had no limits but was personal.

18

The Taking of the Gospel to the Gentiles; Paul

After the resurrection the first followers of Jesus continued to practice traditional Judaism. They still observed the Mosaic Law; they still held that there was only one God and that he had made a special covenant with Israel; they still worshiped in the temple at Jerusalem.

Nevertheless, the early Christians believed that the most important revelation of God was the death and resurrection of Jesus, and this belief subtly altered the traditional Jewish understanding of ethical monotheism and special election. Now the one God was primarily the Father of Jesus who raised him from the dead. Moreover, in some sense Jesus was divine also. Now the ethics of the disciples were primarily the ethics of Jesus, which emphasized the intentions of the heart and the relative unimportance of external obedience to law. Now "election" was primarily being chosen by Jesus and the Spirit and entering into the Christian community. The primary place where God "dwelt" was no longer the temple in Jerusalem, but Jesus' flesh and the church where the Spirit of the risen Christ continued to be present.

Shortly after the resurrection, the early Christians began to preach to their fellow Jews but had only limited success. The Acts of the Apostles tells us that the disciples of Jesus proclaimed to any Jew who would listen that Jesus had risen from the dead and was the prophesied Jewish Messiah. Most people were not convinced.

Jews had difficulty believing that an executed criminal could be the person who God had sent to save them. Not surprisingly, many also opposed a movement that exalted someone who they had helped execute.

Soon a series of events led to the conversion of the first Gentiles. Unfortunately, our knowledge of what happened depends on sketchy and not entirely reliable material in Acts. Nevertheless, the following seems likely. In Jerusalem there was a group of Jews whose first language was Greek and who presumably had lived abroad. Some of them became Christians. They were increasingly critical of traditional Jewish practice, including the Mosaic Law and the temple. Consequently, they were persecuted and fled. They arrived in some of the great Gentile cities of the Roman world, such as Antioch (near the border of modern Turkey and Syria) and Damascus. Since these Jews were fluent in Greek and familiar with Gentile culture, they found it relatively easy to share their faith with Pagans and began to convert them. Soon a considerable number of Gentiles were committed believers in Jesus.

The church in Jerusalem gradually became supportive of Gentile Christianity. The disciples of Jesus had probably always expected the conversion of the Gentile world. Some of the Old Testament prophets had predicted that the entire earth would one day believe in Yahweh and worship at his temple in Jerusalem. Jesus himself had proclaimed that he had come to set fire to the world (Luke 12:49) and that in due time people would come from the "East and the West" and enter the kingdom (Matt. 8:11). Nevertheless, Jesus and the earliest church assumed that the Pagans would become Jews. The sudden appearance of Gentile Christians initially caused confusion. Conservatives insisted that the church must order them to get circumcised and follow the ethnic requirements of the Mosaic Law. Nevertheless, the leaders of the church gradually recognized the validity of Gentile Christianity and encouraged its growth.

We can see the shift by considering the life of Peter. Peter came from a thoroughly Jewish background and had worked as a fisherman on the Lake of Galilee. He became a follower of Jesus in the hope that Jesus would fulfill God's promises to Israel. Apparently, Peter also expected that he himself would share in the resulting earthly glory. Indeed, at least on one occasion, Peter apparently challenged Jesus to begin acting like the Messiah, a challenge to which Jesus responded with bitter criticism (Mark 8:27–38). The Acts suggests that even after Peter had received a resurrection appearance, he along with his fellow disciples still expected Jesus to restore the kingdom of Israel (Acts 1:6). Nevertheless, Peter soon discovered that Gentiles too could receive the Spirit of Jesus, and he began baptizing them. When the church leadership met to consider the question of whether Gentiles could remain Christians without adopting Judaism, Peter supported the legitimacy of Gentile Christianity, and this position prevailed. Subsequently, Peter became a missionary both to Jews and Gentiles. Ultimately, according to church tradition, he even went to Rome, the center of the Gentile world. There he suffered martyrdom.

Nevertheless, the person who was most responsible for making Christianity an international religious movement was Paul. Paul founded and strengthened Gentile churches throughout the Northeastern Mediterranean. He was the most ardent and stubborn defender of the position that Gentiles could become Christians without converting to traditional Judaism by adopting the Mosaic Law. Paul's letters remained influential after his death and ultimately entered the New Testament. His students became church leaders and shaped subsequent Christian generations.

Paul's early life was bicultural and qualified him to help the church make the transition from a Jewish sect to an international religion. His Jewish roots were impeccable. Indeed, he boasted of being a "Hebrew born of Hebrews" (Phil. 3:5). Apparently, he had Jewish parents, and his first language was either Hebrew or its cousin, Aramaic. He had at least his higher education at Jerusalem and became a Pharisee, a specialist in the interpretation of the Mosaic Law. On the other hand, his Gentile roots were impressive also. He was born at Tarsus (e.g., Acts 9:11), an important center of Greco-Roman culture, and he probably received some classical education, since he could write Greek very well. Luke even claims that Paul was a Roman citizen (e.g., Acts 16:37). His dual cultural heritage appears in his double name of Saul/Paul (Acts 13:9). Saul was the first king of Israel; Paul was a common Roman name.

As a young adult, Paul persecuted the church, but we can only conjecture what his specific objections to Christianity were. It is clear that Paul violently persecuted the Christian movement, since both Acts and his own letters repeatedly tell us so (e.g., Acts 9:1–2, 1 Cor. 15:9). Paul records that he acted out of his zeal for the traditions of his ancestors (Gal. 1:14). Doubtless, as a loyal Jew, Paul was offended by the proclamation that a crucified person was the Messiah (cf. Gal. 3:13). He also must have bridled at Christian missionaries winning converts by eliminating Jewish legal requirements. The Christian claim that Jesus was divine would have seemed blasphemous to a Pharisee. Radical Christians were preaching that in Christ Jews and Gentiles were one, and as a Jewish nationalist Paul must have felt most uncomfortable with that assertion. Of course, Paul's need to persecute may also have come from some psychological problem that we cannot reconstruct today.

Paul had a resurrection experience and became a Christian missionary to the Gentiles. It is customary to talk about Paul's "conversion" from Judaism to Christianity, but such terminology is misleading. Paul continued to be Jewish. Indeed, he still observed the Mosaic Law when he was among his co-religionists (e.g., 1 Cor. 9:20). What happened at his "conversion" is that Jesus appeared to him and Paul acknowledged Jesus to be God's "Son." Paul also accepted a commission to preach that the Gentiles could become disciples of Jesus without adopting the Jewish Law (Gal. 1:16).

We can summarize the rest of Paul's life briefly. Immediately after his conversion at Damascus, he went to "Arabia" (e.g., modern Jordan) but does not seem to have made a lasting impact there (Gal. 1:17). He returned to Damascus and briefly visited Peter in Jerusalem and presumably got additional information about Jesus and early Christian tradition. He went to the regions around his native Tarsus (the southeast corner of modern Turkey [Gal. 1:17–21]) and preached. Barnabas, an early Christian leader, invited him to come to the great city of Antioch to assist in evangelism. They worked together there and then went on a missionary journey to Cyprus and Asia Minor. Upon their return Paul discovered that some conservatives were demanding that Gentile Christians get circumcised and follow the Mosaic Law. Paul vigorously objected and went to Jerusalem to seek support for his position that Gentiles could be Christian and still keep their own customs. After some controversy, the leaders of the church supported Paul. He then did more missionary work, especially in the great cities of Corinth and Ephesus, and had considerable success. Unfortunately, when he visited Jerusalem, he was nearly killed by nationalistic Jews who considered him a traitor. He ended up in prison and used his rights as a citizen to appeal for a trial at Rome. After long delays, which he spent in prison, he was finally sent to Rome where apparently he was found guilty (it is not clear what the exact charge was) and executed.

Although it is difficult to be certain, it seems that we can isolate Paul's basic ideas. Paul's surviving letters address specific problems in his congregations and do not present his "theology" systematically. As Paul makes different recommendations in response to different crises, he sometimes justifies his positions in contrasting ways. Consequently, it is not clear what the center of his thought was. Nevertheless, the letters give us many important theological reflections, and we can attempt to arrange them into some kind of coherent whole.

Paul emphasizes that there is only one God, and, through the crucifixion, resurrection, and the giving of Christ's Spirit, God has revealed the final truth. Paul remained a staunch Jewish monotheist, but he now knew God primarily through the great events that brought the church into being. For the Christian Paul, the cross definitively demonstrates God's love for sinners and the wickedness and folly of the world. God loved us enough to have his Son die for us despite our defects. The world is so evil and ignorant that it did not recognize God's Son, but tortured and killed him. The resurrection definitively demonstrates that Christ is mightier than the powers of this age, including death. Jesus now reigns as Lord of all and will soon return in glory. If we live as Jesus did, we will share in his final reign and be transformed into his risen likeness. The Spirit gives us a "down payment" of that final salvation now. As a consequence, we have the paradox of strength in the midst of weakness. As human beings, we are subject to suffering and death and can do little on our own to resist them. Nevertheless, as Christians, we are full of God's Spirit who keeps giving us new resources.

From these basic ideas Paul argues that in Christ there is no Jew or Greek (Gal. 3:28). The fact that there is only one God necessarily implies that he saves both Greeks and Jews without partiality (e.g., Rom. 3:29–30). The cross shows that the Jewish Law that kept Jews separate is foolish, because even the Mosaic Law is part of this world that killed Jesus. The resurrection confirms Christ's triumph over the world and the law. People receive the Holy Spirit not by following the Jewish Law but by listening to Christian preaching, and the Spirit comes to both Jews and Gentiles (Gal. 3:2).

Apparently building on the insights of Jesus, Paul insists that the only ethical requirement of Christianity is to love. Jesus had already taught that the two great commandments are to love God and neighbor (e.g., Mark 12:28–34). Nevertheless, Jesus concentrated on his fellow Jews and assumed that they would also keep the rest of the Mosaic regulations (Matt. 23:23). As a missionary to Gentiles, Paul came to a more radical conclusion. The whole law can be summarized in the commandment to love, and in our relationships with other human beings we owe no one anything except to love each other. The entire law can be summed up in, "You shall love your neighbor as yourself" (Rom. 13:8–10).

A dimension of Paul's thought that would be especially influential in Western Christianity is his claim that law by itself leads to sin and that only faith in Christ can set us free. This claim would become a basis for Augustine of Hippo's (354–430) theology that we cannot choose to do good without first receiving God's grace, and Augustine influenced Western Christianity more than any other post-biblical person. In the sixteenth century, Paul would inspire Martin Luther (1483–1546) and others to found Protestantism on the insistence that we are set right with God only by grace, and we obtain that grace by trusting in God's undeserved forgiveness (see later discussion). Paul continues to impact theologians to the present day.

Here is my personal synthesis of Paul's understanding of the alliance between law, sin, and death and how Christ saves us from it: Paul points out that everyone knows something about the spiritual life. God reveals "his eternal power and deity" (Rom. 1:19–20) in the created world, and in principle everyone can see them. Similarly, thanks to God, we all have at least some "natural" sense of right and wrong (Rom. 2:14).

Nevertheless, human beings do not want to be centered in God, and instead choose to be centered in something else. Human beings resist thanking and praising God for all that we have. We do not wish to live the self-sacrificing lives that ethics demands. Instead we have a deep, corrosive desire to be centered in ourselves, and we look for excuses not to be thankful and moral. As a result, we lose touch with God and decency. This loss of spiritual orientation goes all the way back to the first humans and continues through history. One consequence is that sin is not merely a series of human choices. It is a superhuman power. Only Adam and Eve started with a clean slate. Everyone else is born into a world whose knowledge of God and of morality is already perverted by pride and selfishness. Because we have lost touch with God and decency, we have to live for something else. Whatever we live for is our own debased god. Paul explicitly attacks the Pagan deities of his day. We must remember, however, that the Pagan gods and goddess of the Roman world were basically personifications of such things as sex, wealth, and military strength. Of course, today individuals and groups still can and do choose to live primarily for sexual gratification, money, and the gaining of power through violence.

This destructive orientation distorts first our desires and then our actions and produces death. If we make sex the goal of our lives, we fall into lust and then into promiscuity; if we make money the goal of our lives, we fall into greed and then financial misdoing. When we worship something that is beneath us, we degrade ourselves, and we become obsessed with it, because we are trying to use it to obtain the fulfillment that can only come from doing what is right and loving God. Our sinfulness destroys ourselves and others and inevitably leads to spiritual and even physical death.

We take the first step out of this morass when the "law" confronts us. Due to his Jewish background, Paul concentrates on the biblical code. However, all societies have laws, because without them social intercourse breaks down completely. Paul himself explicitly acknowledges that even Pagans have a "natural" knowledge of moral laws (Rom. 2:14–16). All just laws expose us. They make us see that our obsessive behavior is destructive to ourselves and others and, therefore, is ethically unacceptable. When we make this discovery, our spiritual self rejoices in it. At last we clearly see what is ruining our personal and collective lives and how we need to change.

By itself, however, the law tends to make us worse rather than better. The law tells us that we need to change, but it does not give us the power to do so. We are then tempted to try to save ourselves.

To the extent that we are successful in overcoming our particular faults, we become proud and more self-centered. Nevertheless, Paul assumes that normally we even fail to overcome our specific faults. The reason is that the law undermines our efforts. The law teaches us that we are sinners. The resulting shame makes it even more difficult to achieve spiritual progress. Instead, we end up alienated from ourselves. Our consciences condemn our desires and the actions they produce, our desires rebel, and we disintegrate into internal warfare.

The coming of Jesus enables us to escape from the alliance of law and sin. Jesus reveals God's love for us even when we are trapped in sin and cannot accept ourselves. Jesus invites us to surrender to that love by making God the center of our lives. He founds a community in which his Spirit continues to dwell. Through faith in God's love, we realize that God can do for us what we cannot do for ourselves. By getting baptized and entering the church, we open ourselves to the power of Christ in a community dedicated to his love and service. As a result, we increasingly overcome sin through the Spirit. We are humble and grateful and, spiritually, our self-centeredness dies, and Jesus lives in us.

19

Who Was Jesus and How Can We Know? John's Gospel

The gospels suggest that even during his lifetime, people were puzzled over who Jesus was or claimed to be. We repeatedly read that people attempted to get Jesus to tell them who he thought he was and that Jesus' answers failed to resolve the issue. When Peter declared that Jesus was the Messiah, Jesus responded that Peter was not to say that to anyone because Jesus must suffer (Mark 8:29–31). When John the Baptist sent messengers to ask Jesus if he was claiming to be the one who would fulfill the Old Testament prophecies, Jesus told them to report to John about Jesus' miracles and preaching and added, "Blessed is anyone who is not offended at me" (Matt. 11:6). When he was on trial and the Roman governor asked if he was claiming to be a king, Jesus replied, "That's the way you would say it" (Mark 15:2).

The first three gospels suggest that discovering Jesus' identity was difficult because of contrasting facts. As the inaugurator of God's kingdom, Jesus exercised absolute (i.e., divine) authority. He taught as if he was God, and he worked miracles. Yet, he passed on this authority to his followers. Jesus pointed away from himself to the Father, but in so doing he acted as someone who knew the Father in a unique way and could reveal him.

At the resurrection, it seems that the disciples experienced Jesus as divine. He came to them clothed with divine power and mystery, and through him they received God's own Spirit.

The experience that the risen Jesus was divine raised disturbing questions. Since Jesus of Nazareth was obviously a human being, how could he be divine? When did he become divine? At the resurrection? At his baptism before he began his ministry? At birth? If Jesus was divine, was there really only one God as the Old Testament insists?

In practice the early church made Jesus functionally divine, but this "solution" left important issues unresolved. Thus, Christians insisted that the risen Jesus was functioning as Lord of the universe. Christians also insisted that even during his earthly life Jesus had exercised a power, wisdom, and authority that only God has. However, this practical solution left the crucial questions of whether Christ could really have been human and divine and whether there was only one God unanswered.

These and other issues about Jesus became crucial in the Johannine community because of social problems. The Gospel and Letters of John have great similarities in language, style, and theology and seem to have come from a distinctive movement within early Christianity. From the gospel we learn that "the Jews" expelled the Johannine community from the synagogues and justified this measure by charging that it was blasphemous to claim that a human being was God (e.g., John 10:22–39; cf. 9:22, 12:42, 16:1–4). The Johannine Letters document a schism over whether "Jesus Christ came in the flesh" (e.g., 2 John 7). Apparently, part of the community could not believe that God's Son had the limitations of a human body, and the church split.

John's Gospel responds by trying to give a definitive answer to who Jesus is, how we can know, and why it matters. In this gospel, the recounting of the life of Jesus is primarily a vehicle for telling us who Jesus is and how believing this will lead to our own salvation.

John's Gospel proclaims that Jesus is God incarnate. Already the opening verses insist that before the creation of the world there was an Eternal Word who existed beside God and was himself divine. Indeed, God made the entire universe through this Word. The Word then became "flesh" and was born as Jesus. We find the same insistence that Jesus is God incarnate in the gospel's climax. Jesus demonstrates that even in his risen state he still has a body by challenging a skeptical disciple to feel the wounds left by the crucifixion, and the disciple responds by declaring that Jesus is "Lord" and "God" (John 20:27–28).

According to John's Gospel, it is logically possible for the Son to be divine and yet there only be one God, because the love of the Father and the Son makes them perfectly one. Thanks to their total love for one another, they know each other completely; they give themselves to one another totally; they honor one another fully; they dwell in one another intimately. Because of his love the Son imitates his Father exactly and does everything that the Father wishes. Consequently, the Son mirrors the Father and makes him visible to the world.

The faith that Jesus is God incarnate makes a difference because only if Jesus is fully divine and fully human can he bridge the gap between God and the world. Because Jesus is divine, he perfectly reveals the Father to us (1:18, 14:9), and because Jesus is human, we can receive that revelation fully. We understand a person much more completely than we understand an animal or an angel. Because Jesus is human, his life also can be an example for how humans should think and act. Because Jesus is both human and divine, we can enter into divine life through him. Our friendship with Jesus is friendship with God himself.

John's Gospel insists that its faith in the incarnation arose through an inspired interpretation of the actual past, and it is this interpretation that the gospel provides. John's Gospel acknowledges that it was only after Christ's death and resurrection that the Spirit led the community into all truth (16:12–15). Nevertheless, the gospel also insists that what the Spirit did was to remind the church of what Jesus had said and done and help his followers understand what had actually taken place (14:25–26). The gospel retells the story of Jesus in such a way that we can see the ultimate meaning of Jesus. Thus, the gospel does not simply tell us what Jesus said and did. Instead, it has long sections of interpretation. Especially the speeches of Jesus are not transcripts of Jesus' historical sermons. Rather, they are commentaries from the author of the gospel that explain who he understands Jesus to be and why that understanding is essential for our salvation. We may note in passing that ancient historians commonly wrote speeches to present their understanding of the past and then attributed those speeches to historical characters.

John's Gospel insists that we can verify for ourselves that Jesus is God incarnate as we go through the stages of our own spiritual development.[1] The process begins with the testimony of others and with signs that lead to initial belief. To achieve this belief, all we need do is to accept the invitation to come and see (1:35–51; 4:28–30, 39–42; cf. 7:45–52). Then we will receive convincing signs. This initial faith, however, is undependable (2:23–25). The next step is spiritual rebirth in baptism (2:23–3:21) and the first reception of the Eucharist (chapter 6). To take this step we must make a public confession of our new faith and accept the humbling fact that we must receive the spiritual through material observances. Thanks to the materiality of the sacraments, we will know that God can sanctify matter and, hence, that Jesus had a real body, and that we will rise from the dead. We will revere Jesus as the one who has given us the sacraments and is present in them. The following step is committed discipleship. We must now recognize that despite our growth so far we are still enslaved to sin and still do not know the truth about Jesus (8:31–32). We must also be prepared to suffer rejection from the same world that rejected him. When we become committed disciples, we will have an inner experience that enables us to know that Jesus is God. The process of spiritual growth ends with Christ and the Father dwelling in the believer. This indwelling leads to certainty about God's eternal plan to save the world through the incarnation (14:15–23). To take this final step we need to love as Jesus loved (13:34). When we do this, we participate fully in God's own joy and in some sense become divine ourselves (10:34–36).

John's Gospel has given the church perhaps the most helpful biblical presentation of God's last judgment. The Bible as a whole insists that God punishes sinners. Those parts of the Bible that affirm meaningful life after death predict that there will be a final reckoning, and at it the evil will receive the appropriate penalty. Jesus himself declared that doom awaited unrepentant sinners and used such images as devouring fire and worms to picture it (e.g., Mark 9:47–48). Unfortunately, the church tended to take such images fairly literally and depict hell as a torture chamber. In my opinion, a literal torture chamber would make a mockery of God's forgiveness and compassion for all his creatures. John's Gospel, by contrast, insists that God has no desire to condemn the world. God only wishes to save all that he has made. However, God cannot save us without revealing to us the truth of what we have done and how it has affected everyone else. Such truth is painful, and many people cannot bear it. Hence, they turn away and separate themselves from God's life-giving fellowship and honest relationships with others. As John's Gospel puts it, "All who do what is vile hate the light and do not come to the light lest their works be exposed" (John 3:20). We may assume that "hell" is the final isolation that people experience when they refuse to acknowledge the truth.

NOTES

1. See L. William Countryman, *The Mystical Way in the Fourth Gospel: Crossing over into God* (Philadelphia: Fortress, 1987). I have built on Countryman's work in my own book, *The Past from God's Perspective: A Commentary on John's Gospel* (N. Richland Hills, TX: BIBAL, 2004).

20

The Patristic Era

Around the middle of the second century, the church entered the Patristic Era, which continued until about 500 C.E. We can divide this period roughly into two halves. During the first half, which lasted through 312, Christianity suffered periodic persecution from the Roman government. There had already been occasional persecution in the first century. Nevertheless, these earlier attacks had either come from the Jewish community or else had been a response to alleged crimes that Christians had committed. For example, in the year 64 the Emperor Nero blamed the Christians for a fire in Rome and began executing Christians residing in the city for arson. By contrast, beginning in the second century, being a Christian was itself a crime, and there were periodic government attempts to suppress the church as a whole.

There seem to have been two reasons why the Roman government objected to Christianity. First, Christians in fidelity to their monotheistic heritage would not worship the Pagan deities, which included the goddess Roma and the emperors. To Pagans this refusal seemed both unpatriotic and potentially dangerous to public welfare. Worshiping Rome and the emperor was a tangible sign of loyalty. The refusal to worship the other gods might anger them, and they might visit the entire society with disaster. The second reason that the government objected to Christianity was that the early church in keeping with the teaching of Jesus tended to support social equality. For example, at the Eucharist people from all levels of society shared in a common bread and cup. This egalitarian perspective was threatening to an empire built on slavery and the subordination of women.

In response to the threat of persecution, the church reemphasized its insistence on monotheism but quietly dropped most of its egalitarianism. Despite government warnings and then torture and executions, the church urged its members not to reverence Pagan deities, and many Christians suffered martyrdom. However, to make itself look both respectable and harmless, the church increasingly insisted that its members should take their expected places in the larger society. Slaves were to obey their masters without question; women were to do the same to their husbands. Already by the end of the first century, Christian leaders were urging slaves in their flocks to serve their masters as if serving Jesus himself and urging women to be subordinate to their husbands as the church is subordinate to Christ.

One lasting result of the persecution was the veneration of Christian martyrs and then other saints. To inspire Christians to be ready to give up their lives for the faith, the church celebrated the deeds of those who had already made this total sacrifice. The acts of the martyrs were recorded in writing, and each year the church commemorated the day of their death. The faithful relied on the martyrs to intercede with God in heaven and obtain specific requests. In time the church declared that other Christians who did not die for the faith but had led exemplary lives should also receive veneration as "saints" and could intercede.

After 312 Christianity gradually became the official religion of the empire. In 313 the Roman government officially adopted a policy of religious toleration. Thereafter the Emperor Constantine gave the church more and more patronage and also intervened in its internal affairs. In 330 Constantine moved the capital from Rome to Byzantium (modern Istanbul), which he rebuilt as a Christian city. Constantine received baptism shortly before his death in 337. Under Constantine's successors Christianity became the state religion, Paganism (but not Judaism) was suppressed, and normally the civil government and church leadership cooperated.

A major development during the Patristic Era was the formation of the Christian Bible. Christians had always accepted the Hebrew

Scriptures, which in time were called the "Old" Testament. Ancient Christians also accepted some additional Jewish books that existed in Greek, though there was not complete agreement over which ones, a disagreement that divides denominations to the present day. However, initially there was no explicitly Christian section of the Bible. Gradually the church came to regard early Christian documents as having at least equal authority to the Old Testament. The four gospels and the letters of Paul gained acceptance especially early. Eventually, the church came to nearly universal agreement on twenty-seven books, which were now the "New" Testament. One of the first lists to agree exactly with the ultimate one appeared in 367.

During the Patristic Era, apostolic succession became accepted. During the first two centuries of Christian history there were competing models of church government. For example, the conservative Jewish wing of the church had a dynastic leadership taken from the family of Jesus. In time, however, apostolic succession became the dominant model throughout the church and remains in force for the majority of Christians to the present time.

Apostolic succession holds that only bishops who can trace their lineage back to the apostles have God's approval to lead the church. According to the doctrine, Jesus chose the twelve apostles and gave them spiritual authority. The apostles in turn ordained the first bishops who in turn ordained others, and this succession continues. One must be ordained by a member of this succession to be able to pronounce the forgiveness of sins or celebrate the Eucharist.

In my opinion, apostolic succession remains helpful if we understand it functionally and symbolically. Historically, it seems unlikely that every early bishop could trace his ordination back to an apostle. The early church was too fluid for such a tight succession to be universal. Nevertheless, the original followers of Jesus shaped leading churches, which in turn gave guidance to other Christian communities. Hence, there was continuity between the apostles and subsequent leadership. Such continuity helped guarantee the preservation of apostolic faith and practice. Today apostolic succession remains a powerful symbol of the continuity in church leadership down through the centuries and of a continuing commitment to preserve the apostolic legacy.

Under apostolic succession, the church has three classes of leaders. At the top are the bishops who govern specific geographic areas called "dioceses" and alone have the power to ordain other Christian leaders. Under the bishop are the priests who lead individual congregations and, along with the bishops, have the authority to celebrate the Eucharist and pronounce God's forgiveness to penitent sinners. Finally, there are deacons who assist bishops and the priests, especially in administering baptism and Eucharist and providing relief for the poor and the sick.

During the Patristic period, Christian thinkers used Greek philosophy to try to produce a more systematic understanding of Christian doctrine. In the New Testament era, Christians held many articles of faith, but there was little attempt to think them through and discover how they fit together. In the Patristic period, theologians tended to spell out the precepts of Christian faith rhetorically and tried to show how they cohered.

In trying to produce a "system," theologians frequently resorted to the categories of Greek philosophy, especially Platonism. Platonism, as the name implies, was founded by Plato, an ancient Greek thinker (427–347 B.C.E.). Plato and his followers made major contributions to geometry. Like geometry, the philosophy of Plato assumes that the "real" is the pure concept and that by abstract reasoning we can draw irrefutable conclusions. Thus, in geometry a "real" circle is not something that we can draw but a pure concept. A circle is a set of points equidistant from a single point, and a "point" is infinitely small. By abstract reasoning we can deduce necessary conclusions about a circle, such as how to calculate its exact area. Like the concepts in geometry, the "ideas" or "forms" in Plato's thought are perfect and unchanging. Under the influence of Platonism, Christian theologians thought of God in abstract terms and drew necessary conclusions. Thus, theologians postulated that by definition God is perfect and concluded that, therefore, he cannot suffer, since suffering is a defect.

The previous history of Christianity, beginning with its Old Testament roots, had insisted on, or at least clearly assumed, a series of claims that appeared to be inconsistent. The Old Testament insisted that there was only one God, and the New Testament assumed that Jesus was a human being who, of course, had prayed to God and served him. Nevertheless, the New Testament also held that Jesus was somehow divine and that there was a divine Holy Spirit who dwelt in Jesus and now dwells in the church.

The great theological task of the Patristic era was to come up with models that resolved these seeming contradictions. Specifically, theologians had to explain two things. First, how could the Father (i.e., the one whom Jesus served and to whom he prayed) and Jesus and the Spirit all be divine and yet there be only one God? Second, how could Christ be simultaneously human and divine?

A series of groups in the church produced consistent theologies by denying one or more of these claims. Thus, some groups achieved doctrinal consistency concerning the nature of Jesus by denying his full humanity. The Docetists went to the extreme of denying the reality of Jesus' body. Jesus merely appeared to be human but in fact was a pure divine spirit. The Apollinarians took the more moderate approach of acknowledging the reality of Jesus' body but denied that he had a natural mind and vitality. In Jesus, God's divine intellect and energy substituted for the normal human ones. In contrast to those who denied the full humanity of Jesus, other groups denied his full divinity. Adoptionists held that Jesus was merely a good human being, but as such was all that a human being could be. Thus, for example, some Jewish Christians held that Jesus was a man who kept the Mosaic Law perfectly. The Arians took the more moderate position that Jesus was the incarnation of the greatest creature. Even before making the universe, God had created a supreme angelic Spirit, and this Spirit entered a human life as Jesus. Nestorianism managed to affirm the complete humanity and divinity of Christ by failing to insist that he was fully one person. The Nestorians objected to the pious custom of calling Mary the "Mother of God"; Mary was only the mother of Christ. Finally, the Sabellians managed to affirm that there was only one God and that Jesus was divine by holding that the Father went through two temporary roles in history. He first played the role of Son and then the role of the Holy Spirit.

Ultimately the church rejected each of these positions as heresies. The Greek word from which we get "heresy" meant a "sect" and its special ideology. In Christianity a "heresy" is a wrong opinion that the church as a whole does not accept. The church insisted that the various "heresies" mentioned above were not true to the clear teaching of scripture. Thus, for example, the Sabellian claim that the Father went through the temporary roles of Son and Spirit conflicted with the gospel accounts of Jesus praying to the Father. The heresies also did not adequately explain how humans could become one with God through Jesus. Only if Jesus was fully divine could he fully reveal God to us. Only if Jesus was fully human could he be a model for how we should live. Only if Jesus was fully human and divine could he unite humanity with divinity and redeem us.

At a series of councils the church declared the dogmas (mandatory doctrines) of the Trinity and the Incarnation. The Trinity holds that God is one substance in three persons. God is one reality. Nevertheless, from all eternity he subsists in the Father, the Son, and the Holy Spirit. God the Father eternally begets the Son out of his own substance and breathes forth the Spirit. The Incarnation holds that the eternal Son assumed a human nature by entering Mary's womb and being born as Jesus. In assuming a human nature, however, the Son did not cease being divine. Instead, since the incarnation, he has two complete natures, including both a human and a divine mind and will. Thus, the Chalcedonian definition, which was adopted in 451, holds that Christ is one person in two natures.

A few Christian groups left the larger church as a result of such decisions. Especially in Egypt, some Christians rejected the claim that Jesus had two continuing natures. The Egyptians felt that the Chalcedonian definition did not sufficiently honor the unity of the divine with the human in Christ and verged on Nestorianism. The Egyptians held that it would be more accurate to say that Jesus' human nature was absorbed into his divine one.

For the vast majority of Christians, however, the Trinity and the Chalcedonian definition of the Incarnation became the foundation of "orthodoxy" (correct belief), and in subsequent centuries theologians attempted to explicate these dogmas. As it developed, Christian theology tried to define such vague terms as "substance," "person," and "nature" more precisely. It also tried to explain how the contrasting assertions (e.g., that God could be one substance and yet three persons) could all be true simultaneously.

Unfortunately, unquestioned assertions based on Greek philosophy doomed this effort from the start. Such philosophical categories as substance, person, and nature could not adequately capture the realities either of human life or of divine revelation. Even more serious, the unquestioned assertions that God could not change or suffer excluded the logical possibility of incarnation and crucifixion. To become human and die on the cross, God necessarily had to change and suffer. The orthodox reply that God only changed and suffered in his human body and mind made little sense. If the Son took on a human life, then the divine Son himself must have changed by adopting a body and mind and must have felt the pain of crucifixion.

In modern times, theologians have shown that we can affirm the Trinity if we adopt a different set of philosophical assumptions. Following Donald Gelpi,[1] I would hold that the best model for God is a supremely perfect community. In a human community, persons simultaneously become distinct as they develop their individuality and become united as they work together in love. The primary human reality is community, not isolated individuality, because we only realize our potential through interacting with others and working as one. Typically in a human community some people concentrate on reflection; others, on the basis of that reflection, make decisions; still others carry out the decisions; and through this cooperation we make our greatest accomplishments. Since, according to Genesis 1, God made us in his own image, we should think of God as analogous to a human community. In the Trinity the Father is the source of the godhead. The Son is the one through whom the Father and the Spirit act. The Spirit is God's mind. These three become persons through giving themselves to each other. For example, the Father is a complete person, because he can think and act. He thinks through the Spirit and acts through the Son. Consequently, the Trinity does consist of three persons in one God. The Trinity also provides a model for how we as human beings should live together. We must become fully loving communities in which all the members become complete persons by sharing their special gifts with each other and working together as one.

Following Gelpi, we can also affirm the Chalcedonian definition. The incarnation took place when a divine person, the Son, chose to have a human experience. The Son ruled the human experience that we know as Jesus of Nazareth. In other words, the thoughts and actions of Jesus were the Son's own thoughts and actions. Consequently, since the incarnation the Son is one divine person who is both fully human and fully divine. The eternal Son continues to be the divine person who sustains the universe. Nevertheless, the Son also experiences firsthand the limited life of Jesus as his own life. In Jesus the Son can only think and do the things that are possible for a human being. As a result, we can, for example, affirm that since the incarnation the Son has both a divine and a human mind. As the Son, he continues to know all things through his divine mind, which he has thanks to his fellowship with the Spirit. He also has the limited human mind of Jesus, and through that limited mind, he reveals to the world all of God that a human life can express.

NOTES

1. See, especially, Donald L. Gelpi, S.J., *The Divine Mother: A Trinitarian Theology of the Holy Spirit* (Lanham, MD: University Press of America, 1984), 125–143, 161–166.

21

Monasticism

Once the Roman persecutions ended and the emperor became Christian, the church faced a new threat of worldliness. Of course, during the persecutions, people did not join the church to seek economic or social advantage. The church was almost by definition counter-cultural. The threat of martyrdom meant that every Christian was committed, and there often was no need to do anything "extra" to show one's total devotion to God. After the emperor became Christian, the situation changed drastically. Vast numbers of people converted merely out of conformity or even to better their worldly position. Such people often did not significantly change their self-indulgent lifestyles. The church as the "official" religious structure seemed to endorse the legitimacy of corrupt political and social systems. Bishops in major cities had governmental power and oversaw large sums of money and sometimes became venal. Hence, to an alarming degree the church no longer challenged people to repent and lead self-sacrificing lives in the service of God and others.

Christian monasticism arose in part as a reaction to this worldliness. Many people felt that everyday life in the church could no longer express full devotion to God. Something more was needed and they became "monks."

We may define a "monk" as a celibate who leaves normal life to devote his or her life to prayer and works of mercy. Thus, a monk is not necessarily ordained. Most monks are lay persons. Nevertheless, a monk cannot be someone who usually lives a "regular" life and merely spends more time than most people in prayer or social outreach. Instead, a monk must be single and visibly abandon conventional society.

There are two basic types of monks. Eremitic monks reside alone, though they welcome temporary visitors and give spiritual advice. Cenobitic monks live with one another in communities. The communities can be loose, consisting of hermits living in close proximity and interacting. More frequently in church history, the communities are monasteries in the proper sense, that is, communities that have a common worship, work, and table.

An important founder of monasticism in Eastern Christianity was Antony of Egypt. Antony lived an extraordinarily long life, since he was born around 251 and did not die until 356. Consequently, he himself experienced the transition from persecution to establishment. At one point in the earlier part of his life, he actually visited and encouraged Christians who were in prison or were serving as slave labor in the mines. Yet, well before his death Christianity had become the dominant religion in the Roman Empire. Antony came from a wealthy Christian family and inherited an estate. Nevertheless, in response to Jesus' summons in the gospel to give up possessions, stop worrying about material things, and follow him, Antony distributed his property to the poor and devoted himself to prayer and fasting. He spent long periods in solitude at various locations in Egypt, a burial vault, an abandoned fort, the bottom of a mountain in the desert. Ultimately, the holiness of his life attracted many who wanted to share his spiritual zeal. Antony counseled and encouraged them. In his Life of Antony, Athanasius records that Antony did battle with demons who tormented him and often appeared in bizarre shapes, such as strange animals. It is hard to know how to interpret this material today. On the one hand, one can see these experiences as mere hallucinations brought on by solitude and fasting. On the other hand, one can note that when we devote ourselves to meditation, the negative feelings that we have previously repressed surface powerfully, and we must struggle with such things as anger and lust directly. In any event, Antony became adept at distinguishing good "spirits" from evil ones. Good spirits give us peace, whereas evil ones produce fear and anxiety. Antony also stressed that the monk can banish the demons, especially by turning to God in prayer.

Partly due to the inspiration of people like Antony, there arose a movement of desert monasticism. Under a variety of leaders in Egypt, Palestine, and Syria, a large number of Christian hermits lived in the wastelands. It is noteworthy that some of the desert monks were women. Collectively these early figures are known as the Desert Fathers (and Mothers), and many of their sayings about the spiritual life have survived and continue to inspire people today.

In Western Christianity, the most important founder of monasticism was St. Benedict of Nursia (c. 480–c. 550). As a young man, Benedict studied at Rome and then, in reaction to the immorality of the times, withdrew to a cave where he devoted himself to prayer. He soon attracted disciples, and he organized them into monastic communities. Ultimately, he founded the famous monastery at Monte Cassino in southern Italy. Benedict composed an influential monastic rule. The Rule of St. Benedict was based on various earlier rules but strove for moderation. Benedict self-consciously wanted a way of life that a normal person could tolerate. The Rule mandated that one third of a monk's time should be devoted to prayer, one third to work, and one third to rest. The most important activity of the monastery was the saying of eight daily worship services, which came to be known as the liturgy of the hours. Ultimately, the Rule of St. Benedict became the basis for thousands of monasteries in Europe and elsewhere.

During the centuries of chaos that followed the collapse of the western half of the Roman Empire, monasteries kept civilization alive. The monks preserved ancient learning by copying books and providing education. Monks also made important intellectual advances that laid the foundation for subsequent progress. We may especially mention the monastic development of plain chant and then harmony in music. In the visual arts, monasteries produced illuminated manuscripts that contained both highly decorated letters and separate illustrations. Some of these manuscripts, such as the Book of Kells (c. 800) and the Lindisfarne Gospels (c. 715), remain among the greatest treasures of world art.

Within cenobitic monasticism women sometimes rose to prominence. As we noted above, women had played an important role already in the desert hermit movement. In cenobitic monasticism, monasteries for women (often called nunneries or convents) appeared. For example, while Benedict was founding communities for men, his sister Scholastica was apparently doing the same for women. Nunneries had their own female heads (abbesses) and could become large and influential. Sometimes male and female communities associated. In such cases the leader of the joint community might be a woman. For example, Hilda of Whitby (614–680) founded and ruled over a large double monastery in England and even helped train many men, some of whom later became bishops.

One of the greatest medieval abbesses was Hildegard of Bingen (1098–1179). She corresponded with political and church leaders and was one of the most accomplished persons of her era. She wrote on a variety of fields, including theology, medicine, botany, and geology. She was particularly famed for her visions. Today she is principally remembered for her music and art. Her innovative musical compositions and illustrations remain among the finest of her period and continue to be popular.

Unfortunately, ultimately some monasteries became wealthy and worldly. Monasteries made money through a variety of activities, such as farming and the production of books. In addition, Christian individuals as an act of piety would give property to monasteries. Since the monastery as an institution could continue indefinitely, some monastic orders gradually became rich. As a result, monasticism sometimes became an illustration of worldliness and privilege, instead of a protest against them.

Despite such problems, monasticism remains an important part of Christianity even today. Monasteries provide communities of public worship and private prayer that lift up the needs of the church and the world to God. These communities also offer places where Christians living in the conventional world can go on retreat and cultivate the life of the spirit. In addition, some monastic orders continue to foster scholarship and education and do exemplary charitable work among the poor and the sick.

22

Three Major Types of Christianity

During the controversies about the Trinity and the nature of Christ, a few Christians broke with the winning party and formed independent traditions that still exist today. Here we may especially note the coptic churches in Egypt and Ethiopia that rejected the theological formulation that Jesus had two continuing natures.

Nevertheless, the vast majority of Christians accepted the ancient decisions of the ecumenical (world) councils. Indeed, those decisions were seen as the foundation of "orthodoxy."

Subsequently, however, for both theological and geopolitical reasons, Christianity divided into three major traditions: The Eastern Orthodox, the Roman Catholic, and the Protestant, and we will now summarize the origins and special characteristics of each.

EASTERN ORTHODOXY

The Eastern Church gradually became distinctive. The Pagan emperor Diocletian, who reigned from 284 until 305, divided the Roman Empire, producing eastern and western administrative units. In the fourth century, Constantine became the first Christian ruler of the empire and began to give the church imperial patronage. He also moved the capital east from Rome to Byzantium, which was more defensible, and made it a Christian city. The older western half of the empire collapsed under the onslaught of invading Germanic tribes in the fifth century. By contrast, the Eastern Empire endured until 1453. It was in the context of the Byzantine Empire that Eastern Christianity took on its special characteristics. The political and cultural situation in the east differed greatly from the west, and the Eastern Church evolved accordingly. Subsequently, missionaries spread the faith into Russia and elsewhere. The usual name for this Christianity is "Eastern Orthodoxy."

Ultimately, primarily for political reasons, Eastern and Western Christianity officially split. Because the Emperor Constantine had transferred the capital from Rome to Byzantium, Byzantium saw itself as the New Rome. Consequently, chronic disputes erupted over the relative authority of the popes, the leaders of the old Rome, and the leaders of Byzantium. Sometimes formal relations broke down completely. For example, in 1054 the pope's representative excommunicated the leader of the Eastern Church who then excommunicated the pope. Shortly thereafter the crusades sealed the schism (and permanently alienated the Islamic world). Byzantium itself initially asked for the west to send crusaders to deal with the military threat from Islam, but things went awry. As western Christians attempted to conquer the "Holy Land," they killed many Muslims and eastern Christians. Then when the crusaders temporarily gained control over areas that traditionally had been under eastern bishops, they substituted western ones. The native population never accepted this political and religious imperialism. In 1204 the crusaders even seized and pillaged Byzantium itself and ruled it until 1261. Eastern Christians became bitter and subsequently rejected high level attempts to restore unity with the west.

Because the split occurred after the controversies about the Trinity and the nature of Christ, there is little difference in doctrine between Eastern and Western Christianity. Only on a small number of points have the east and the west had open theological contention, and these appear to be minor. The most famous and important disagreement concerns the procession of the Holy Spirit. The Latin (western) creed declares that the Spirit proceeds from the Father *and* the Son, whereas eastern theologians insisted that the Spirit proceeds from the Father *through* the Son. It is far from obvious that this issue is of critical significance. Moreover, when we talk about God, our language is at best approximate, and "from the Son" and "through the Son" may amount to the same thing.

The primary difference between Eastern and Western Christianity is one of emphasis in worship, spirituality, art, and political involvement. The east has less stress on political activism. Unlike in the west, Eastern Christianity was beholden to the emperor throughout its formative period. Consequently, the church normally could not effectively criticize government policies, and a strong tradition of the church advocating justice for the poor and the oppressed did not develop. The Eastern Church does, however, have a long tradition of providing charitable relief to the needy.

Eastern Christianity especially focuses on the adoration of God and resurrection of Jesus. Byzantine worship centers on praise and concentrates on the heavenly Christ who rules the universe. As a consequence, the ritual is solemn and magnificent. Eastern Christianity places a special emphasis on Jesus' resurrection, since it was the occasion on which Jesus triumphed over death and returned to heavenly glory. Easter is the focus of liturgy.

With the emphasis on the resurrection of Jesus, there is a corresponding emphasis on our transformation into the divine likeness of the risen Christ. The name for this transformation is divinization. Divinization begins already in this life. God created human beings in his own image, and through the incarnation God united himself to humanity. Consequently, human beings have a natural orientation to God, and as we grow in the Christian faith, God increasingly fills us with his divine glory. This process culminates in eternal life when we shall be fully changed into the likeness of the risen Christ.

The eastern emphasis on adoration helped lead to a greater stress on the mystery of God and the limits of speculative theology. In the west theologians had more confidence in their ability to understand the divine through abstract reasoning based on philosophical presuppositions. By contrast, eastern theologians tended to stress that God is too great for human minds to fathom and in his "essence" is unknowable. Hence, while the east emphatically affirms the central doctrines of Christianity, such as the Trinity and the incarnation, it has been less willing to explicate them in detail. We come to know God primarily through adoring prayer rather than through rational reflection.

The eastern emphasis on adoration may in part be due to historical circumstances, but it also expresses a fundamental truth both about God and the spiritual life. Historically, Byzantine society paid extravagant homage to the emperor. God naturally was viewed as an even greater emperor, one worthy of endless praise. Nevertheless, adoration is essential to Christianity. God is supremely praiseworthy. He is total love, total power, total knowledge. Human beings internalize these truths through adoring him. Psychologically praise centers us in God and helps overcome the basis of all sin, self-inflation. Since God loves us, we must also assume that our praise brings him joy.

In church art and architecture adoration led to the dome, the mosaic, and the icon (painted image). Eastern Christian art has to reflect the majesty of the risen Christ and the glory of the saints who have been divinized. Eastern Christianity has little sculpture, since sculpture emphasizes limited space and cannot do justice to the divine. Orthodox churches normally feature a dome covered with mosaics or icons representing Jesus, Mary, saints, and angels. The dome draws us to contemplate heaven. There is also an iconostasis, a wall of icons that separates the congregation from the altar where the Eucharist is consecrated. Symbolically, this wall marks the border of heaven, and its pictures become windows through which we gaze into eternity.

Eastern Christianity has also produced what is probably the most profound theology of Christian painting. Eastern Christianity stresses that God as he is in himself is beyond representation. Consequently, the Father is ordinarily portrayed in some form that he temporarily assumed when he communicated to humans in the biblical stories. Icons find their theoretical justification in the doctrines that God became human in Jesus and that people who follow Jesus are transformed into his divine likeness. Icons reveal the presence of God shining through Jesus, Mary, the saints, and angels and also make them visible to us. Thus, through the icon we make deeper contact with heavenly realities, and these transform us.

Because of this theology, icons tend to have the following characteristics. Icons have relatively few details, so that the worshiper is not distracted. They also avoid "realism" so that they point us to heavenly realities and remind us that these differ greatly from the earthly realm that we know. Icons are beautiful so that we can experience the transcendent beauty of Jesus and the saints and be transformed into their likeness. Icons are expressive so that we can experience the compassion and righteousness that dwell in God's heart. Icons have inverse perspective (i.e., the picture seems to move forward into our space) so that God confronts us as much as possible. In icons the light seems to come from within the image rather than shine on it from outside to remind us of the presence of God's light within Jesus and the saints.

The supreme architectural monument of Eastern Christianity is the Church of the Holy Wisdom which was completed in 537 and is now a museum in Istanbul. Justinian (483–565), the most powerful of the Byzantine Emperors, had the huge building erected. Its most magnificent and innovative feature is the central done which rests over a set of windows and seems to have nothing supporting it. The church symbolizes not only the earthly glory of Justinian but also the awesome mystery and grandeur of the invisible God.

ROMAN CATHOLICISM

The bishops of Rome increasingly assumed leadership over Western Christianity. Throughout the Roman Empire the churches in large metropolitan areas became increasingly influential, especially when they could make the prestigious claim of having been founded by an apostle. In the east a number of these churches, especially Antioch and Alexandria and then Byzantium, vied for leadership. By contrast, in the west the church at Rome enjoyed a unique status. As the traditional capital of the empire, the city of Rome had unparalleled political and social importance. Both Peter and Paul had gone to Rome and suffered martyrdom there. No other church in the western half of the Roman Empire could claim to be apostolic. At first the Christian community in Rome consisted of independent house churches, but in the second century Rome began to have a monarchical bishop with administrative authority over all congregations. This bishop came to have the title "Pope" ("Father"). In the subsequent controversies about the Trinity and the nature of Christ (see earlier discussion), the prestige of the Roman church increased as the popes supported positions that ultimately prevailed. When the Roman government in the west collapsed as a result of Barbarian invasions in the fifth century, church officials—and, especially, the popes—helped fill the void. In time the popes became the temporal rulers of Rome and central Italy. Even today the section of Rome known as the Vatican City is a sovereign nation with the pope as its head. The popes sent missionaries to convert Northern Europe. Thus, for example, Pope Gregory the Great (c. 540–604) sent Augustine of Canterbury (d. c. 605) to evangelize England. Of course, the missionaries whom the popes sent encouraged their converts to look to Rome for guidance.

Meanwhile the popes made ever greater claims of spiritual and administrative authority based on Peter. The popes increasingly asserted that Jesus entrusted the leadership of his church to the apostle Peter (see esp. Matt. 16:13–20 and John 21:15–19). In papal teaching, Peter was the first bishop of Rome, and the popes as his successors inherited his authority. A major part of this authority is the power to pronounce forgiveness of sin (including remitting God's punishment for sin) and to make laws regulating the life of the institutional church and its members. Ultimately, these claims culminated with universal jurisdiction and papal infallibility. Universal jurisdiction means that the pope as the leader of the church has the responsibility to appoint and supervise all other bishops and choose some bishops to be cardinals who elect the next pope. Infallibility means that the Papacy is incapable of error when solemnly pronouncing major dogma in behalf of the church. It must be emphasized, however, that an individual pope does not have personal infallibility. Instead, the Papacy as an institution is infallible when, speaking for the church, it formalizes what the faithful as a whole already believe. Thus, the infallibility of the pope is an expression of the infallibility of the church.

Roman Catholics are those Christians who acknowledge the leadership of the Papacy, and today they are especially numerous. Historically, most Eastern Christians rejected the growing claims of the popes and particularly objected to papal infallibility. The east felt that only a general council of church leaders should declare dogma, and only dogmas that were subsequently accepted by the church as a community were infallible. In the west, however, most Christians accepted papal claims, at least until the Protestant Reformation in the sixteenth century. Subsequently, despite the Protestant revolt, the majority of Christians continued to acknowledge papal leadership. Thanks to the heroic work of Catholic missionaries and to Catholic countries conquering other lands, the faith has spread through much of the world, and today Roman Catholicism is by far the largest denomination.

Aside from the claims about the Papacy, the differences between Roman Catholicism and Eastern Orthodoxy mostly involve distinctive emphases. For example, Catholicism has always been politically active, especially in championing of the needs of the oppressed. As we saw above, Eastern Christianity quickly became politically subservient to the emperor and was usually unable to criticize government policies. By contrast, in the west the Papacy was politically independent. This independence allowed—indeed, often required—political activism. An especially attractive part of this activism has been a continuing emphasis in church preaching and theology that governments must be humane and provide for the poor and the helpless. At various times and places the Catholic Church has directly attacked oppressive and callous government policies.

Another major difference is that Catholicism has placed greater stress on the crucifixion of Jesus and the human sin that led to it. In Eastern Christianity, the dominant image of Jesus was the risen Lord. By his resurrection Jesus conquered sin and death and now reigns over the universe. Roman Catholicism, by contrast, has traditionally placed a stronger emphasis on the sufferings of Jesus. For example, one of the most popular Catholic devotions for centuries has been the stations of the cross, in which the faithful meditate on different moments in Jesus' passion from his condemnation to his burial. The emphasis on the cross encouraged reflection on the human sinfulness that led to the torture and death of the innocent Jesus. The Catholic Church stressed the depth and pervasiveness of human sin and emphasized that Jesus overcame sin by paying the price for our wickedness. Consequently, the confession of sin and the request for God's forgiveness have traditionally been central to Catholic private devotion and public worship. In Christian art, Roman Catholicism has especially produced paintings and statues of Jesus on the cross.

The Catholic Church decisively influenced the course of western music. Catholic monasteries led the way in developing harmony. Subsequently, the Catholic Church was for centuries the most important musical patron. Some of the greatest composers of all time, such as Palestrina (1525–1594) and Mozart (1756–1791), worked for the Church and produced enormous amounts of liturgical music, especially settings for the Mass.

In the visual arts Catholicism has been remarkable for the diversity of its contribution. Whereas Eastern Christianity encouraged only a narrow range of styles in only a few art forms, Catholicism down through the centuries sponsored various movements in stained glass, sculpture, painting, and architecture.

Many people would hold that the greatest era of Roman Catholicism was the high Middle Ages (roughly 1000–1350), and in any event, this period produced extraordinary achievements that remain decisive for Catholicism today. By the end of the tenth century, political stability began to return to Western Europe. A new optimism prevailed. With this new optimism a succession of great theologians argued that the truth of Christianity was compatible with reason. Of these thinkers the most influential was Thomas Aquinas (c. 1225–1274). Aquinas attempted to synthesize all of theology. In his work he argued that many important truths about religion (e.g., the existence of God) could be demonstrated by philosophic reason. Other truths (e.g., the Trinity) could only be known through revelation. Nevertheless, even these revealed truths could be analyzed and explicated. Ultimately, Thomas' thought became authoritative for Catholicism and remained so up to the Second Vatican Council (1962–1965).

In the visual arts, the most important development was Gothic architecture, which many consider to be the supreme artistic achievement of Christianity. The Gothic style originated in Paris in the middle of the twelfth century and then spread throughout Western Europe. For more than a century, huge Gothic churches rose everywhere. Aesthetically, the primary goal of the Gothic style was to use stained glass to produce an inner illuminated space. The transfigured light symbolized the presence of God. To allow for as much glass as possible, Gothic relied on such architectural elements as the pointed arch and the flying buttress.

Nevertheless, the supreme artistic symbol of Catholicism is the church of St. Peter's in Rome. This church was (re)built in the sixteenth and seventeenth centuries. It was the largest church in the world and symbolized the authority of the Papacy. The architects and decorators included some of the greatest in Christian history. Bramante (1444–1514) drew up the original architectural plans. Michelangelo (1475–1564) designed the dome. Bernini (1598–1680) produced the colonnade and interior furnishings. St. Peter's remains a center of pilgrimage to this day.

PROTESTANTISM

Protestantism arose as a "protest" against the abuses of the imperial Papacy. Etymologically, the word *Protestant* is related to the word *protest* and originally meant to "testify" for the truth. By the beginning of the sixteenth century, the Papacy had become thoroughly worldly. Popes obtained election through bribery. The popes ruled central Italy and participated in the Machiavellian diplomacy of the era. Some popes led immoral personal lives, engaged in extravagant nepotism, or sold church offices. A particularly severe abuse was the hawking of indulgences, which the faithful bought to ransom loved ones from purgatory (a place where the dead suffered temporarily for their sins before entering paradise). Much of the money from selling the indulgences was going to pay for St. Peter's, the most costly church in the world (see earlier discussion).

The founder of Protestantism was a German biblical scholar, Martin Luther (1483–1546). Luther first attacked the sale of indulgences. He went on to break with the Papacy over larger theological issues, especially his claim that Christians are saved by God's undeserved mercy, which we receive through faith alone. Jesus on the cross paid the penalty for our sins. In grateful trust we must simply accept this undeserved gift. Thus, Christians do not earn salvation through good works and certainly cannot purchase it through indulgences. Instead, we do good works in thanksgiving for the undeserved salvation we have already received. The papacy excommunicated Luther, and he and his followers became a separate Christian denomination.

Protestantism has always been diverse. Once Luther inaugurated his protest against Roman Catholicism, other leaders such as John Calvin (1509–1564) and Ulrich Zwingli (1484–1531) followed. While these men agreed on "justification by faith" and the rejection of papal authority, they disagreed on Eucharistic doctrine. Luther favored consubstantiation; Zwingli, memorialism; and Calvin, something in between (for an explanation of these terms, see pages 76–77). Different denominations arose, especially the Lutherans who, as the name implies, followed Luther, and the Reformed Churches who followed Calvin. More radical groups, such as the Anabaptists and the Baptists, rejected infant baptism and government oversight of religion. In subsequent centuries all these groups continued, and still more movements came into existence, such as the Pentecostals, who revived the ancient Christian practice of ecstatic speech and other charismatic gifts. In addition, the government-sponsored church in England (and its territorial possessions) combined elements of Catholicism and Protestantism to produce a "middle way."

Because it began as a protest against Papal abuses, Protestantism has emphasized the opposite side of religious life from Catholicism. After the Protestants broke with the Papacy, they became polarized and rejected anything that could be seen as specifically Catholic ("Papist"). This rejection then became the basis for a continuing Protestant tradition. Thus, for example, the Catholic church supported monasticism and required all clergy to be celibate, and as a Catholic Luther had been a monk. After he broke with the Pope, Luther left his monastic order and married. Subsequently married clergy became the norm in all Protestant denominations. The Catholic (and Eastern Orthodox) Church had an Old Testament that contained not only the Jewish scriptures but also later writings. Luther and the other Reformers revised the Old Testament, declaring that these later books were not authoritative, even if they were worthy of being read. This shortened canon became universal in Protestantism, whereas the Catholic and Eastern Orthodox Churches retained the longer one. Today most Bibles print these disputed books in a separate section called the Apocrypha.

Protestantism emphasizes the authority of this revised scripture as opposed to the authority of church tradition. Over the centuries Catholic theology and practice evolved, and Luther and other early Protestants concluded that Christianity had become corrupted. Hence, Protestants attempted to return to what they perceived to be a more authentic faith and life. To find this earlier and purer religion, they relied on the Bible and insisted that it alone was normative and must take precedence over later tradition. An early Protestant slogan was "by scripture alone." The Bible contained everything that was necessary for Christian salvation. Subsequently, Protestants have always stressed that doctrine and worship must be based on "God's Word." Hence, for example, Protestants reject the Catholic practice of praying to the Virgin Mary and the saints, because it cannot be found in the Bible.

Protestantism also emphasizes the authority and freedom of the laity. In Catholicism the authority of the ordained hierarchy is virtually unlimited, and the clergy have special sacramental powers. The individual Catholic obtains salvation by obeying the dictates of the hierarchy, conforming to accepted church belief and behavior, and receiving the sacraments. In reaction to this emphasis on the corporate church and the authority of its ordained leaders, Protestantism has always stressed the individual and the laity. All Christians should read the Bible for themselves and not simply accept the interpretation of church leaders. People must come to an individual faith based on personal study and experience. Protestantism grants lay people a voice in church government. In the past the civil rulers of an officially Protestant state sometimes regulated church affairs. In more recent times, congregational democracy has become more common. Church members decide policy and choose leaders by elections in which each person in a congregation has a vote. At least in many Protestant groups (e.g., the Baptists) the local congregation is virtually independent. Protestant clergy do not receive special ("magical") sacramental powers through ordination and do not claim to be part of a self-perpetuating dynasty ("apostolic succession") going back to the time of Jesus. Protestants rely on the free forgiveness of God experienced personally rather than on the obtainment of a priestly absolution.

Protestants favor simplicity in public liturgy in contrast to the more elaborate rituals in the Catholic tradition. Protestants have tended to be critical of grand worship, because they felt that excessive ritual and pomp inflate the clergy. Protestants also felt that the many rites of traditional Catholicism encouraged superstition. Worship should be transparent, plain, and focus on the reading and explication of scripture. As a consequence, Protestants have in practice emphasized preaching rather than the Eucharist. The sermon was the center of liturgical life. From the beginning Protestants insisted that worship must take place in the common language of the people, whereas Catholicism kept the Mass in Latin until the nineteen sixties.

One unfortunate result of its insistence on simplicity in worship is that Protestantism has not made as great a contribution to the visual arts as Catholicism. The simpler worship of Protestantism did not accommodate painting and sculpture. Moreover, since art was a fundamental part of much Catholic tradition, Protestants tended to dismiss elaborate art as "Papist." Protestant churches normally had little or no ornamentation. Consequently, artists in Protestant communities needed to rely on secular patrons and produced fewer religious works. Nevertheless, Rembrandt (1606–1669), a member of the Reformed Church, painted some of the most profound Christian pictures, and in recent times Protestants have become more supportive of religious art.

In contrast to its relative neglect of the visual arts, Protestantism has always made fundamental contributions to church music. Luther wrote hymns, and congregational singing became central to Protestant liturgy. Hymn singing helped inspire Protestants to produce musical works that were as grand and complex as those of Catholic composers. Many would consider the musical compositions of the Lutheran Johann Sebastian Bach (1685–1750) to be the greatest in Christian history. The "Messiah," by the Protestant composer George Friedrich Handel (1685–1759), is perhaps the most beloved major piece of sacred music in English.

Protestantism has on the whole been more responsive to change than Catholicism and Eastern Orthodoxy, and this responsiveness has, in my opinion, been both a blessing and a problem. Since it downplays tradition, Protestantism has often been more open to new developments in human knowledge and social organization. Such openness allowed at least many Protestants to accept more quickly progress in such things as biblical studies and the liberation of women. On the other hand, without the restraining influence of tradition, Protestantism has also fallen prey to fads and would-be prophets. These have fostered splits within existing denominations and led to a proliferation of small sects. There are now over two hundred Protestant groups.

23

The Challenge of Modernity

One immediate result of the rise of Protestantism was a long period of violence. In the name of Jesus, Catholics and Protestants fought a series of brutal wars. The resulting suffering was often horrendous. For example, in the last of these conflicts, the Thirty Years War (1618–1648), perhaps a quarter of the population of Germany perished. Even in peaceful times, Catholics and Protestants also regularly tortured and killed one another.

The violence led to increased hatred, and consequently, even when the worst abuses ended, extreme polarization between Catholics and Protestants persisted. The polarization lasted well into the twentieth century.

Because Catholics and Protestants could not live together in charity, there began to be separation of religion and politics. As long as a state was officially Catholic or Protestant, it would persecute citizens belonging to the other persuasion. Hence, thinkers began to urge that the state should not have an official religion but should remain neutral and guarantee the rights of individuals to practice different faiths. Especially in the United States, which subsequently had more and more influence on the larger world, religion was disestablished. In theory, at least, the government became wholly secular.

One unfortunate result was that religion often came to be seen as a subjective, "inner" experience, and Christians had more difficulty obtaining political reform. Religion, it was increasingly felt, had to do with one's personal relationship with God. It was an individual activity, and it should not enter into public discourse. Consequently, it became harder for Christian groups to criticize governmental sin and demand change effectively.

During the same period, there were profound breakthroughs in the sciences and the humanities that raised questions about earlier Christian belief. Modern astronomy and paleontology disproved the literal truth of the opening chapters of Genesis. Modern scientific biblical studies disproved the literal truth of many of the stories about the history of Israel, the life of Jesus, and the early history of the church (e.g., that the twelve tribes of Israel literally came from the twelve sons of Jacob). Previously, some Christians had regarded the Bible as infallible, and all Christians had assumed its basic accuracy. Science also raised questions about the usefulness of religion for averting natural disasters. Christians had thought that God directly caused lightening strikes, plagues, and similar catastrophes. These expressed his anger. Religion was essential to placate God and protect society from the dire consequences of divine displeasure. Now science demonstrated that lightening was nothing more than static electricity and that microbes, not God, caused epidemics. Consequently, the new breakthroughs in knowledge threatened many people's faith.

In response to these disturbing discoveries, some Christians affirmed outdated perspectives, while others abandoned the core doctrines of the traditional religion. In reaction to the increasing skepticism that new discoveries were producing, some Christians debunked science and scientific history. Many aggressively insisted on the literal truth of the entire Bible. Others affirmed traditional church teaching as incapable of serious error. Such biblical and ecclesiastical "Fundamentalists" continue to be numerous today. By contrast, other Christians enthusiastically accepted the "scientific" conclusions and became skeptical about the most central traditional beliefs. One such group is the Unitarians, who have rejected the Trinity and the divinity of Christ.

One helpful result of the discoveries of modern times was that now Christians could abandon predestination. Previously Christians felt compelled to affirm that God knew precisely what each person would do. God, by definition, was omniscient, and the

Bible clearly taught that the prophets of the Old Testament had foretold in detail what would take place centuries later. Unfortunately, the belief that God knew in advance what human beings would do seemed to imply that we do not actually have the freedom to make meaningful choices. Instead, the God who created us had determined our actions beforehand. Theologians also assumed that God had to punish people for evil deeds. Hence, many Christians, especially in the Reformed Churches, even affirmed that God predestined people to everlasting damnation. The discoveries of modern times eliminated the need for such dire conclusions. Modern biblical studies showed that the Old Testament prophets spoke about their immediate future, and that some of their predictions did not turn out to be accurate. Modern philosophy held that we create the future by our free choices. Hence, it is not a defect in God's omniscience if he does not know what we will do. There is nothing to know in advance. Consequently, even in the Reformed tradition, talk of predestination—especially predestination to damnation—disappeared.

Meanwhile anti-Christian movements arose and sometimes persecuted Christians. Of these movements, communism was especially powerful, widespread, and violent. Under communist regimes atheism was the official government ideology, and public education labored to instill it in the young. Church activities were often severely restricted. People who insisted on visibly practicing their faith suffered discrimination and could not get into universities or obtain the better jobs. In some cases Christians were arrested and sent to labor camps or executed. Fortunately, in the last years of the twentieth century, the majority of communist regimes disappeared or became tolerant of religion.

As modern communications and travel developed, Christians came into increasing contact with the great spiritual traditions of Asia, especially Buddhism and Hinduism. Already in the sixteenth century Roman Catholic missionaries arrived in India and Japan and encountered Asian religion. Of course, as European nations asserted increasing control over such places as Indochina and India, the contact between eastern and western religion became constant.

In response to these developments, mainline Christians began to advocate closer cooperation among different denominations and dialog with non-Christian religions. The "ecumenical movement" especially labored to get Protestants, Catholics, and the Eastern Orthodox to stop attacking each other and come to agreement about various theological issues, such as the nature of the Eucharist. Different Christian communities also increasingly worked together to promote common social goals, particularly the relief of the needy and the promotion of political rights. Institutional structures arose to facilitate such cooperation, especially the World Council of Churches, a consultative body that came to include many Christian groups. Various churches began to have serious exchanges with representatives of other religions. Such contacts included theological discussions that explored common beliefs and ethical commitments. Sometimes Christians and non-Christians even prayed or meditated together.

The rise of gay and lesbian liberation movements has raised a new and divisive issue in the church. Traditionally, the church seldom discussed homosexuality. This silence reflected a consensus that gay and lesbian sex was too obviously sinful ("unnatural") to require serious consideration. The Old and New Testaments have a couple of texts condemning homosexual conduct as especially offensive (e.g., Rom. 1:24–27), and in subsequent church history, whenever theologians bothered to discuss same-sex activity, they condemned it. The church also supported the prosecution and punishment of active homosexuals. Consequently, for century after century, gay and lesbian persons kept their personal lives secret and did not raise larger ethical issues. One ironic result was that some clergy were practicing homosexuals, but the larger church usually overlooked this fact. Recently in response to growing tolerance from the secular world, gay and lesbian Christians have broken their long silence. They now vocally emphasize that their sexuality can express deep love and can be the basis for monogamous unions. The New Testament, beginning with Jesus himself, insists that the ultimate test of whether behavior is Christian is whether it expresses genuine, committed love. Therefore, the church should now recognize gay unions as legitimate and even produce "marriage" ceremonies to bless them. In response to these developments, a few churches (including my own) have begun to ordain openly gay people and to perform single-sex wedding ceremonies. Other Christian groups have emphatically reaffirmed the traditional teaching that homosexuality is sinful.

It can be said in summary that the modern period has been one of great ferment and struggle for Christianity, but also one that seems to be bearing much fruit. In some areas church attendance has declined severely. For example, many Western Europeans have abandoned Christianity altogether, and many more only regard Christianity as part of their national heritage. Yet, there have been enormous advances in theology, some of which we see in earlier discussion. Christianity remains the largest religion on earth, and in some traditionally non-Christian areas (e.g., China), the church has mushroomed. Best of all, the church as a whole seems to have grown spiritually. We may especially rejoice that the church is now determined not to repeat the worst mistakes of the past. Today no Christian denomination would endorse persecuting the Jews or starting a war against other Christians in the name of Jesus or imposing "white" Christianity on another culture (see later discussion). Indeed, various church leaders have publicly apologized for such tragic historic abuses.

24

The Feminine in Christian Tradition

Christianity originated and evolved in patriarchal societies. Israel, from which Christianity took much of its heritage, was highly patriarchal. For example, women could not be priests and could only inherit property under unusual circumstances. Menstruation made females temporarily unclean, and during their period they could not go to the temple. The Greco-Roman world in which Christianity first became popular was patriarchal too.

Consequently, Christianity itself has traditionally been patriarchal. God was portrayed in male imagery, especially, as a "Father," even though theologians taught that God "himself" has no sex. Ordained church leaders were always men. The church told women to defer to their husbands.

Monotheism reinforced the patriarchy of Christianity (as it also did in Judaism and Islam). Polytheism allowed for the existence of female deities as well as male ones. In such a complicated religious system, opportunities existed for women to serve as priestesses, and a given individual could choose to render special devotion to a goddess. By contrast, in Christianity monotheism led to a consistently patriarchal structure.

To some extent, the patriarchy of Christianity was further reinforced by the incarnation. God became incarnate as a male human being, Jesus. Jesus then became a model for priesthood and a theological argument for restricting ordained ministry to males.

Nevertheless, there was always an important feminine dimension to Christianity. A couple of books in the Old Testament, especially Ruth and Esther, are the stories of heroic women. A few of the prophets in the Old Testament were women. The Old Testament portrays God's "Wisdom" as a wondrous woman. As such she guided God in the creation of the world. She is present in all things. She invites the foolish to come and learn. Through this learning we can find such blessings as prosperity and health. Wisdom even becomes an object of mystical devotion. The Old Testament also portrays Israel as feminine. The nation is the bride of Yahweh. In keeping with that heritage, the New Testament and subsequent Christianity pictured the church as a woman, the bride of Christ and the mother of the faithful. Jesus himself had, at least for his time, a shocking openness to high status for women. In a patriarchal culture that prohibited women from religious study, Jesus had women students who even traveled around with him. He reached out to marginal women, especially the physically and mentally ill whom he healed, and to socially despised prostitutes. He proclaimed that in God's kingdom (which Jesus was inaugurating) the last would be first, and the "last" apparently included women. All these "feminist" dimensions to Jesus' life and teaching led to criticism, including the thinly veiled allegation that he was a playboy. After the resurrection, women discovered that the tomb of Jesus was empty and apparently were the first to meet the risen Lord. As a result, a few women were even "apostles" by the original definition of the word (i.e., someone to whom the risen Christ had appeared and given the command to proclaim the good news of the resurrection). At least a few women subsequently became prominent as missionaries. Thus, in her own day Prisca (Priscilla), along with her husband, shared with Paul the honor of founding the important church at Corinth. She (and her husband) also did missionary work at Ephesus and Rome and, apparently, was regarded as Paul's equal. The gospels, especially Luke and John, normally portray women in the most sympathetic terms and emphasize their role in the life of Jesus and, by implication, the early history of the church. Many women, such as Perpetua and Felicitas, suffered martyrdom during the Roman persecutions and were honored as saints. Churches were dedicated to them. With the establishment of Christianity as a state religion in the fourth century and the rise of monasticism, some women became prominent in the church either as empresses/queens or as abbesses of monasteries (see earlier discussion), and some of these figures too ultimately were canonized. For example, two Byzantine empresses, Irene (c. 752–803) and Theodora (c. 810–862), played a crucial role in officially reestablishing the use of icons after a period of bitter controversy and are honored as saints in the Eastern Orthodox tradition. Women made especially important contributions in spiritual writing. The church pictured the soul as feminine, and patriarchal society was relatively tolerant of women writing on devotional subjects. Partly as a result, down through the centuries a series of women, including Julian of Norwich (1342–c. 1420), Teresa of Avila (1515–1582), and Evelyn Underhill (1875–1941), produced some of the most profound and influential books on the life of prayer. Fairly quickly in church history, however, the principal feminine dimension to Christianity was the increasing veneration of Mary, the mother of Jesus. In the earliest Christian tradition, Mary played only a minor role, in part because she apparently had not believed in Jesus during his ministry (esp., Mark 3:21, 31–34). Mary did, however, become a disciple after the resurrection (Acts 1:14). The Gospel of Luke devotes a large section of its opening two chapters to Mary, especially her willing consent to God's invitation to become the mother of his Son. In Luke, Mary is the first disciple of Jesus and provides a model of ideal discipleship.[1] In the Gospel of John the dying Jesus tells Mary and the evangelist that they must now be respectively mother and son, and we read that subsequently the evangelist took her into his own home (John 19:26–27). Thus, symbolically Mary and the evangelist fulfill the highest Christian calling, namely becoming Christ for one another in this world. As church history continued, Mary played a larger and larger role in Christian devotion, especially among ordinary believers. An important watershed occurred in 431 when the Council of Ephesus confirmed the legitimacy of the popular practice of calling Mary the "Bearer of God" (in the west, "Mother of God"). Mary was viewed as an efficacious intercessor with Jesus. The faithful would present their needs to Mary and ask her to intercede with her divine Son. Many believed that Mary was the mediator of all graces. In public liturgy Mary became especially prominent in Roman Catholicism. Mary was frequently invoked in Masses. The words of and to Mary in Luke 1–2 became a major part of liturgies in monastic communities. Among the laity, the Rosary ultimately became the most popular devotion, and the Rosary consisted of the mantra-like repetition of central texts, some of which came from the words to Mary in Luke 1 and meditations on scenes in the history of salvation, especially scenes in which Mary was present. A major part of popular religion came to be centered on appearances by Mary at places such as Walsingham (1061), Guadalupe (1531), Lourdes (1858), and Fatima (1917), and Catholics especially thought of Mary as their spiritual "Mother." Ultimately, the Catholic Church declared a series of dogmas that exalted Mary. The Church decreed that Mary shared with Jesus the unique honor of being born without original sin. Underlying this declaration was the further belief that Mary had not sinned subsequently. The church also held that Mary had always remained a virgin and at her death had been taken up bodily into heaven. Mary also became a favorite subject in church art and music. Paintings of Mary—especially ones in which she was with the infant Jesus—became especially common.

It would appear that the traditional veneration of Mary fulfilled historical and psychological needs. Historically, the veneration of Mary provided a Christian alternative to the veneration of female deities in the Pagan world. Psychologically, Mary provided reassurance of mercy and forgiveness. In a patriarchal culture, where the ideal man was a warrior, an athlete, or an ascetic, men were supposed to be demanding and "just." Mercy and compassion were "feminine" qualities. Consequently, Jesus and God the "Father" tended to be seen as stern. Mary filled the gap by providing access to mercy and forgiveness. She had endless compassion and would intercede with God and Jesus for her sinful children. We must also assume that psychologically, Mary provided a helpful devotional image to people who had destructive relationships with their fathers but good ones with their mothers.

At present the veneration of Mary is controversial, since some wish to expand it, whereas many others feel it should be reduced. Thus, on the one hand, some Roman Catholic conservatives hold that Mary shared with Jesus the supreme honor of redeeming the world. Mary freely consented to become the mother of God's Son and thereby enabled the incarnation. She also shared in Christ's atoning suffering as she witnessed the crucifixion. Hence, she is a "co-redemptrix." There has even been a movement to have this claim become part of official Catholic teaching. On the other hand, Protestants have always regarded the veneration of Mary in Eastern Christianity—and especially in Roman Catholicism—as excessive and complained that it detracted from the centrality of Jesus. Liberal Catholics wish to place more emphasis on scripture, where Mary plays a much smaller role than in subsequent church tradition.

Modern scholarship has cast doubt on the virginity of Mary. Specialists in scripture argue that the New Testament calls into question the historical accuracy of the perpetual virginity of Mary, since it seems to indicate that Mary had other children after Jesus. The traditional arguments that these younger "brothers" and "sisters" of Jesus were from a previous marriage by Joseph (the Eastern explanation) or refer to "cousins" (the classic Catholic explanation) seem forced. More radical scholars would even question whether the virgin birth of Jesus is historical, since the early church could easily have imagined it. The Roman world believed that various great men had been born of virgins. Matthew was probably the first writer to assert that Jesus was born from a virgin, and Matthew explicitly cites an Old Testament prophecy that a future Jewish king would be born from a virgin (Matt. 1:22–23; Isa. 7:14). It is noteworthy that the word *virgin* only appears in the Greek translation that Matthew was using, not the original Hebrew. Moreover, when Matthew and Luke record that Jesus was born of a virgin, they are primarily making a theological claim about Jesus' unique relationship to God, not a historical statement about Mary's sexual abstinence.

The traditional picture of Mary does not appear to have been liberating for women. A virgin mother cannot be a model for other females. Consequently, the veneration of Mary did not necessarily increase respect for women in general. In practice the emphasis on Mary's perpetual virginity tended to demean sexuality, particularly female sexuality. The tradition stressed the utter obedience and humility of Mary. No matter how much Mary was exalted, she was always totally subservient to God and Jesus, and they were pictured as male. Hence, in practice the adoration of Mary encouraged women to accept oppression.

Although Protestant groups historically lacked feminine devotional images, Protestants led the way in ordaining women. Because Protestantism focused on scripture rather than tradition, there was no veneration of the saints, and consequently, the great women of church history received little attention. Protestantism's relative lack of concern about church tradition and openness to innovation, however, made it easier for women to become church leaders. From their beginnings radical groups, such as the Quakers, gave women full equality with men, and in recent times an increasing number of Protestant denominations have started ordaining women as pastors and raising individual women to ever higher leadership roles. My own denomination, the Episcopal Church in the United States, began ordaining women priests in the 1970s, and, as of the date of this book, an ordained woman is the leader of my church as a whole.

Today many would argue that what especially needs to be done is to image the Holy Spirit as feminine.[2] In the Old Testament the Spirit is feminine, since the Hebrew word for spirit ("ruah") is a feminine noun, and "She" is closely associated with God's Wisdom who, as we see in earlier discussion, is customarily pictured as a wondrous woman. As Donald Gelpi has stressed, the symbols that scripture and church tradition use for the Spirit tend to be psychologically feminine. The human mind makes unconscious associations and, as a result, certain things are archetypally masculine and feminine. Water and doves, for example, have female associations because of the water of the womb and the fact that birds lay eggs. And water and the dove are major symbols of the Spirit in Christianity. Indeed, the gospels record that at the baptism of Jesus, the Holy Spirit in the form of a dove alighted on Jesus as he came up from the water (e.g., Mark 1:10).

In my opinion, the following is the way forward as the church seeks to honor the feminine dimension of Christianity. We need to recover a devotion to the Holy Spirit and use feminine imagery to portray her. We should picture the Holy Spirit as our "Divine Mother" (Gelpi) and see the love of God as being like a mother's love, as well as a father's. We ought to think of Mary as an icon of the Holy Spirit. Most of the New Testament texts that mention Mary portray her as somehow a vessel of the Spirit. For example, we read that she conceived Jesus by the Holy Spirit (Matt. 1:20,

Luke 1:35). Whereas Jesus is the incarnation of the Son, Mary, like every Christian, was transformed by the Spirit. As an icon of the Spirit, we should see Mary's acceptance of Jesus as a model for our own lives whether as men or as women. We must see the incarnation of God as a male human being not as an invitation to oppress women, but as a demand that males especially imitate the self-sacrifice and generosity of Jesus "and his willingness to treat women as equals of men."[3] We need to place greater emphasis on powerful women saints as role models. An especially important female saint is Mary Magdalene. She was a prominent disciple of Jesus during his lifetime. He healed her of a severe nervous disorder ("seven demons"; Luke 8:2). She helped bankroll his ministry (Luke 8:3). She accompanied him to Jerusalem and witnessed the crucifixion and burial (e.g., Mark 15:40, 47). She discovered the empty tomb and received a resurrection appearance in which she was told to convey the good news to the other disciples (e.g., Matt. 28:1–10). As a result, she was by definition an apostle (someone who received a commission from the risen Lord to proclaim the resurrection). Even in patriarchal church tradition, Mary Magdalene was exalted as at least "equal" to the apostles. We must also include women in every level of leadership in the church. My own church now has female deacons, priests, and bishops, and they have added immeasurably to our common life.

NOTES

1. See Raymond Brown, et al., eds., *Mary in the New Testament: A Collaborative Assessment by Protestant and Catholic Scholars* (Philadelphia: Fortress, 1978), 105–177.
2. Donald L. Gelpi, S. J., *The Divine Mother: A Trinitarian Theology of the Holy Spirit* (Lanham, MD: University Press of America, 1984), 215–238.
3. Gelpi, *The Divine Mother.*

25

Post-European Christianity

Christianity, of course, originated as a Middle Eastern religion. Its ultimate roots were in the experience of the Israelites who were racially and linguistically a Semitic (Arab) people. Jesus, the founder of Christianity, was racially a Semite, spoke a Semitic language, Aramaic, and lived in Palestine. All of Jesus' disciples were Semitic.

In subsequent centuries, Christianity spread to various areas, and many of the resulting churches have maintained their distinctive heritages until today. Thus, Christianity quickly came to such diverse places as Ethiopia, Armenia, and India, and these ancient communities continue to exist.

Nevertheless, the Christian movement became centered in Europe due to a series of historical accidents. As a result of the Jewish revolt (66–70 C.E.), Jerusalem, the birthplace and initial center of Christianity, was destroyed. The city was subsequently rebuilt and ultimately became a pilgrimage site, but it never recovered its original prominence in Christianity. Even during the lifetime of Jesus, Israel was under European (Roman) rule, and the dominant languages of the Roman Empire were European, Greek in the east and Latin in the west. One consequence was that the Christian Scriptures (as opposed to the scriptures that Christianity took over from Judaism) were in Greek. Paul and other missionaries quickly established Christianity in the great cities of the Roman Empire, and many of these cities were in Europe. When the Roman emperors became Christian, they began to exercise supervision over the church, and the emperors were European and reigned from the great European cities of Rome and Byzantium. As a result, these capitals became the administrative centers of Christianity. Subsequently, European Christianity sent missionaries north who ultimately succeeded in converting all of Northern Europe. Meanwhile, in the seventh and eighth centuries, Islamic armies conquered northern Africa and the Middle East, greatly weakening the ancient Christian communities there. In some areas Christianity disappeared altogether, and in others (e.g., Egypt) Christians ultimately became only a small minority.

Beginning with the Renaissance, European cultures began a long conquest of the rest of the world. Because of continuing scientific and technological advances, Europe increasingly had a decisive military advantage. One result was that European nations made contact with the entire rest of the planet and overwhelmed most of it. From the middle of the sixteenth century through the middle of the twentieth, the bulk of the planet belonged to European empires or spheres of influence.

The subjugated peoples often had little choice but to "convert," and initially had no real understanding of Jesus' message. Sometimes the Western conquerors simply imposed Christianity. For example, Catholic Spain forced native peoples in the "New" World to adopt the national religion. As late as the nineteenth century, the government of the United States outlawed native religions on Indian reservations. But even when the adoption of Christianity was "voluntary," the native peoples often accepted it primarily to curry favor with the conquerors or as part of a larger effort to assimilate. All too frequently, there was little awareness of God's special love for the marginal. Instead of God being the champion of the oppressed, he was seen to be the patron of an oppressive system.

While "imported" Christianity ultimately became central to the lives of many of the conquered peoples, the resulting churches often did not fit well with the cultures as a whole. Naturally, the forms of Christianity that Europe imposed reflected the unique cultural achievements and limitations of the European experience. The conquered usually forgot their pre-Christian religions. Nevertheless, in other ways, the native population remained loyal to its ancient heritage, which conflicted with European Christianity. A schizophrenia arose. On Sunday people went to church where they looked at European art that portrayed Jesus as white. They listened to European music and heard theology expressed in the academic categories of European philosophy. Sometimes church services were even in a European language that the natives did not speak or fully understand, such as Latin or King James English. The rest of the week, however, people continued to live much as they always had with their own art, thought, and speech.

One consequence was that Christianity produced racial and cultural alienation. People imagined that Jesus was somehow European and that their own races and cultures were inferior. God preferred Caucasians and European customs and regarded others as somehow dirty or ugly. Such alienation made people ashamed of their racial appearances and contributed to a neglect of native achievements.

In response to these problems, there have always been efforts to inculturate Christianity and make it non-colonial, and these efforts have been frequent recently. From the beginning of colonial contact, some innovative Christian missionaries incorporated native traditions into worship, and courageous individuals such as Bartolome de Las Casas (c. 1484–1566) opposed oppression. Especially in modern times, some Christians have struggled to make use of native traditions to express the Christian message. The church has encouraged local artists to work in native styles and portray Jesus and the saints with the racial characteristics of the populace. Worship takes place in native languages. Theology is expressed in the images and thought forms of the general population. The church becomes a champion of attempts to obtain political and social justice for oppressed aboriginal peoples. Churches even enter into dialog with surviving non-Christian religions and philosophies.

One thing I discovered from personal experience is the futility of trying to go back to some allegedly pure pre-European culture. It is tempting to try to return to the way things once were. Nevertheless, this attempt is doomed from the start, because with the introduction of European Christianity a new, more complex culture appears, and soon this culture is all that any living person has ever known. Hence, any attempt to return to a forgotten past produces yet another round of alienation, as I myself learned firsthand.

When I briefly took over a church in Barbados, I found out that the wholly black congregation was outraged that the previous priest had taken down some very European statues and the mahogany arch that supported them. The priest was attempting to make the church interior reflect the native cultural heritage. The congregation angrily responded that the statues and arch were part of their heritage. People had grown up with them, and their grandparents had sacrificed to pay for them!

The way forward is to seek a new cultural synthesis that honors as much of the diverse past as possible. The church must not abandon those aspects of European culture that have become deeply rooted in popular consciousness and remain genuinely helpful. Yet, the church must get beyond European perspectives that degrade native peoples by making them feel inferior. Churches must honor native cultural traditions and practices that are compatible with Christianity. We must, however, recognize that much of native culture has also been oppressive (to women, for example) and should not become part of church life.

Getting to this synthesis is neither fast nor easy, but we must persevere. Each step of the way is an experiment, and some experiments fail. Still, we must not give up but continue to invite the Holy Spirit to guide us in inculturating the gospel despite all the difficulties. As we invite God to guide us, we can take comfort in the memory that he also guided Israel and the church through millennia of conflict, change, and growth. And by the crucifixion and resurrection, he showed for all time how great his power is and how great his love.

Index

Abelard, Peter, 85–87
Abraham, 11–12, 16
Adam and Eve, 1–3, 7–8, 10, 19, 56, 85, 109
Adoptionists, 121
Amos, 29–30
Anabaptists, 138
Antiochus Epiphanes, 39–40
antisemitism, 84–85, 145
Antony of Egypt, 126–27
apocalypticism, 39–41
Apocrypha, 138
Apollinarians, 121
apostles, 148, 153
apostolic succession, 119, 139
Aquinas. *See* Thomas Aquinas
Arians, 121
Ark of the Covenant, 16, 19
Armenia, 155
ascension, day of, 97; ascension of Jesus. *See* Jesus, ascension of
Athanasius, 126
atheism, 88, 143
atonement, doctrine of, 85–88, 101; moral exemplary theory, 87; penal substitution theory, 85–87; physical theory, 85–86; ransom theory, 85–87; satisfaction theory, 85–87
Augustine of Canterbury, 134
Augustine of Hippo, 108

Bach, Johann Sebastian, 140
baptism, 9, 44, 54–57, 85, 110, 114; of infants, 56–57, 138; of Jesus. *See* Jesus, baptism of
Baptists, 138–139
Barabbas, 84
Barnabas, 106
Bartolome de Las Casas, 157
Benedict of Nursia, 127–28; monastic rule of, 127
Bernini, 137
Bible, xi, 1–3, Old Testament, xi, 118–19; New Testament, xi, 119, 105; individual books of the Bible. *See* titles (e.g., Gospel of John)
bishops, 119–20, 125, 134
Bramante, 137

Brown, Raymond, 153n1
Buddhism, 70, 87, 143

Calcedonian definition, 122–24
Calvin, John, 137–138
Catholicism. *See* Roman Catholicism
China, 145
Church of the Holy Wisdom, 133
circumcision, 56, 104
Communism, 143
confirmation, 56
Constantine, 118, 129–30
consubstantiation, 76–78, 138
Coptic churches, 129
Countryman, L. William, 115n1
covenant, at Sinai, 16–17, 76; new covenant, 19, 75–77
creation, 1–6; stories of, 1–3; doctrine of, 3–6
crucifixion of Jesus. *See* Jesus, crucifixion of
Crusades, 130

Daniel, book of, 40
David, 24–25, 49–50
deacons, 120
Desert Fathers and Mothers, 127
diocese, 120
divinization, 131
Docetists, 121

Easter, 93, 97–99, 131
Eastern Orthodoxy, 19, 129–36, 138, 140, 144, 149, 151
Ecclesiastes, book of, 33–34
Ecumenical movement, 143–44
Egypt, church in, 122, 129, 156
Elijah, 19
England, Church of, 138
Episcopal Church, 152
Essenes, 73
Esther, book of, 148

Ethiopia, 129, 155
Eucharist, 54, 73–79, 114, 118–20, 139, 144
Exodus, the, 15–20; book of, 15–20, 100–01
Ezekiel, 27

faith, 6, 12–14, 69, 108, 114
The fall, 7–8, 10
First Corinthians, 75–76, 92–93, 101
Fundamentalists, 5, 142

Gelpi, Donald, S.J., 52, 123, 124n1, 152–53
Genesis, 2–3, 5, 7, 10–12, 15, 17
Gnostics, 3–5
God, doctrine of, 3, 5–6, 10, 13–19, 22–23, 25, 27–31, 35–36, 51–52, 61, 103, 147; name of, 15, 17
Gospels of Matthew, Mark, Luke, and John, 43–44, 66, 111; Gospel of John, 44, 50–51, 76, 98–100, 112–15, 148–49; Gospel of Mark, 43, 66, 68; Gospel of Matthew, 49–51, 95, 98, 100, 151; Gospel of Luke and the Acts, 49–51, 95, 97–99, 103–07, 148–51
Gothic, 136
Gregory the Great, 134

Handel, George Friederich, 140
heresy, 121
Herod Antipas, 55, 82
Herod the Great, 49–50
Hilda of Whitby, 128
Hildegard of Bingen, 128
Hinduism, 70, 87, 143
Holy Spirit, 49, 55, 95, 97–103, 107–08, 121–24, 152–53, 158; procession of the Holy Spirit, controversy over, 130–31
homosexuality, debate over, 144
Hosea, 29–30

icons, 132–133, 149
incarnation, doctrine of, 19, 51–52, 76, 85–88, 112–14, 122–23, 131, 147, 153
India, 155
indulgences, 137
infallibility of the pope, 134
Irene, Empress, 149
Isaac, 11–12
Isaiah, 27
Islam, 12, 130, 147, 156

Jacob, 11, 15
Jeremiah, 27
Jesus, ascension of, 97–101; as role model, 13, 101; baptism of, 54, 112, 152; birth of, 49–51; crucifixion of, xii–xiii, 35–36, 52, 63, 81–89, 106–08, 112–13, 123, 135, 158; life of, 43–45, 155; personality of, 45–46; resurrection of, xii–xiii, 6, 36, 40, 51, 55, 70–71, 91–103, 107–08, 111–13, 131, 135, 148, 158; support of women, 148; teaching of, 39, 59–64, 111, 114
Job, book of, 34–36
John's Gospel. See, Gospel of John
John the Baptist, 44, 54–55, 66–67, 111
Jonah, 30–31
Joseph, father of Jesus, 49–50
Joshua, 22; book of, 22–23
Josiah, 25
Judaism, 12, 18, 38, 100, 103, 147
Judges, book of, 22–24; period of, 22–24
Julian of Norwich, 149
Justinian, 133

Kells, Book of, 127
Kingdom of God, 59–64, 70, 74, 78, 81, 111

last judgment, 114–115
last supper, 75
Law of Moses, 16, 18–19, 37–38, 103–06, 108
Letters of John, 112
Lindisfarne Gospels, 127
liturgy of the hours, 127
Lord's Prayer, 59, 61
love, duty to love God, 19, 108; duty to love other people, 19, 61, 83, 86–87, 89, 108, 114; God's love for us, 18, 86–87, 110; love of the Father and the Son for each other, 113
Luke–Acts. See Gospel of Luke and the Acts
Luther, Martin 108, 137–38, 140
Lutherans, 138, 140

Maccabees, the, 39
Manasseh, 25
marriage, 53–54; proposed marriage ceremonies for homosexuals, 144
Mary, the mother of Jesus, 49–50, 121, 139, 149–53
Mary Magdalene, 91–93, 98, 153
Meier, John P., 65, 67, 71–72n1–3
memorialism, 77–78, 138
Michelangelo, 19, 137
miracles, 5–6, 22; of Jesus, 45, 59–61, 65–72, 82, 90, 111–12
monasticism, 125–128, 138; eremitic, 126; cenobitic, 126–128
monotheism, 2–3, 19, 38, 88, 103, 107, 112–13, 117–18, 147; and the problem of undeserved suffering, 88–90
Moses, 15–17, 19–22, 37–38, 100–01; Mosaic Law. See Law of Moses
Mozart, 136

Nero, 117
Nestorians, 121
Nicene Creed, 51
Noah and the Ark, 10

ordination, 53
original sin, 8–9, 12, 56

Palestrina, 136
Passover, 15, 83
Patristic era, 117–124
Paul, 12, 36, 51, 55, 75–76, 99–101, 105–10, 133, 155
penance, 54
Pentecost, 97, 99
Pentecostals, 138
Perpetua and Felicitas, 148
Perry, Charles, 95, 96n1
Peter, 104–106, 111, 133–34
Pharisees, 73, 100, 105
Philippians, Paul's letter to, 51, 100
Plato, 120
Platonism, 120
Pontius Pilate, 83–84
pope, 133–134
predestination, 142–143
priests, 120
Prisca, 148
prophecy, biblical, 27–31, 39–40, 50, 102, 104, 111, 143
Protestantism, 129, 134, 137–41, 144, 151–52
Proverbs, book of, 33–34
purgatory, 137

Quakers, 152

Reformed Churches, 138, 140, 143
Rembrandt, 140
Resurrection, of Jesus. *See* Jesus, resurrection of; of all the dead, 39–40, 55, 59, 78, 100, 114
Roman Catholicism, 129, 133–41, 143–44, 149–51

rosary, 150
Ruth, book of, 148

Sabbath, 2, 97
Sabellians, 121–122
Sadducees, 73, 100
Saint Peter's Church in Rome, 136–37
saints, veneration of, 118, 139, 148–49, 152–53
Sanders, E.P., 90n1
Satan, 34, 59, 61, 85–86
Saul, the first king of Israel, 24, 105
Scholastica, 128
Sermon on the Mount, 46
Solomon, 24–25
stations of the cross, 135
Strauss, David, 67–68
Sunday, 97

tabernacle of Moses, 16
Teresa of Avila, 149
Theodora, Empress, 149
Thirty Years War, 141
Thomas Aquinas, 136
Thomas, Gospel of, 47n1
Transfiguration, the, 19–20
transfinalization, 77–78
transignification, 77–78
transubstantiation, 77–78
Trinity, 5, 19, 55–56, 122–23, 131, 133, 136, 142
Tutu, Desmond, 20

unction, 54
Underhill, Evelyn, 149
Unitarians, 142

wisdom, biblical, 33–36, 148
World Council of Churches, 144
Wright, N.T., 39, 41n1, 61, 64n1, 73, 79n1, 82, 90n2

Zwingli, Ulrich, 137–38

DATE DUE

Demco, Inc. 38-293